DON'T SWEAT
THE SMALL STUFF
FOR TEENS
JOURNAL

DON'T SWEAT
THE SMALL STUFF
FOR TEENS
JOURNAL

RICHARD CARLSON, PH.D.

HYPERION

New York

ISBN: 0-7868-8765-6

FIRST EDITION

10 9 8 7 6 5 4 3 2 1

CONTENTS

DON'T SWEAT

THE SMALL STUFF

FOR TEENS

JOURNAL

1

DON'T THROW UP ON
YOUR FRIENDS!

※ If you had the flu, you wouldn't throw up on your friends, would you? Of course not! So why do we emotionally throw up on our friends? When a bad mood strikes, or we are about to lose it emotionally, we should keep our distance from friends and family so we don't infect them. But instead, we sometimes throw up on them by unleashing all our negative thoughts and insecurities on them. While you may hate the world on Monday, you'll probably love it on Tuesday, so spare everyone the emotional throw-up—your low moods will pass.

What can you do instead of throwing up on others? Try these suggestions to help the negative emotional times pass.

1. Hang a "Do Not Disturb" sign on the door to your room and spend some time alone with your favorite music or a funny movie.
2. Exercise. Even if you're not already practicing a regular routine, a simple walk can help.
3. It sounds very New Age, but try some deep breathing exercises: Sit quietly, close your eyes, inhale slowly, hold it for a second or two, and exhale slowly. Clear your mind while you do this. Do at least five minutes of deep breathing.
4. Learn yoga! Get a videotape or a book, and practice this amazing combination of exercise and meditation. Everyone is doing it—they can't all be wrong!
5. Write about how you feel. It can help a lot to put feelings down on paper. Even if you write "I feel rotten, I feel rotten, I feel rotten" over and over, it can help you release that feeling.

6. Hug your pet or favorite stuffed animal. Better yet, try talking to your pet. Talking to an animal who will just listen can sometimes take the weight of the world off your shoulders.

7. What's your favorite thing to do to relax? Make your own list of things to do, then do them. You'll soon feel better, and when the moods pass, you can visit with your friends and family again.

2

CONVINCE YOURSELF THAT
ONE TEEN DOES
MAKE A DIFFERENCE

❋ Many teens think they couldn't possibly make a difference in the world, but the truth is that you can! Actions that are thoughtful, helpful, cooperative, generous, and kind don't have to be monumental to make a difference. You can help one person at a time. You'll be surprised at how good it makes you feel, too.

Are you ready to start? Here are twenty simple things that you can do to give of yourself, help others, or promote a cause. This week, try to do at least one thing, and check it off. Next week, try another, or maybe two. Each time you do something on the list, check it off. Be creative—come up with more ways to make a difference in the world and add them to the list.

_____ Do volunteer work for an organization that supports a cause you believe in, like an animal shelter, a hospital, or a sports league for kids.

_____ Help someone who's having a tough time with schoolwork.

_____ Write a note to someone special, just to tell him or her that you think he or she is special.

_____ Smile at kids you don't know at school.

_____ Pick up some litter.

_____ Clean out your closet and give good but unused items to charity.

_____ Do a helpful chore for an elderly neighbor or family member.

_____ Stand up for a friend who is being picked on.

_____ Call someone you haven't talked with for a while and catch up.

_____ Send a thank-you note for a gift.

_____ Invite someone new to your next gathering of friends.

_____ Be there for someone who needs a shoulder to lean on.

_____ Fix something that's broken.

_____ Help with a household chore.

_____ Give your folks a night off by baby-sitting for your younger sister or brother.

_____ Help raise money for a good cause.

_____ Do something good for the environment.

_____ Buy canned food with some of your allowance, and then donate it to a food bank.

3

DON'T SWEAT THE BREAKUPS

✳ Yes, breaking up is hard to do—and very hard to get through emotionally. You're devastated, you feel as if you're absolutely going to die, and you swear that you'll never get over it or meet anyone else. Breakups are an essential part of life—otherwise, we'd all end up marrying the very first person we were ever interested in! Put breakups in perspective by remembering the good times, forgetting the bad and angry feelings, and wishing the other person well.

Need some help putting your breakup into perspective? Write down positive thoughts about yourself. Include things you like about yourself, why you deserve to be loved, and what you can give another person. Next, write down positive thoughts about your former partner. You don't have to be angry at the other person or harbor thoughts of revenge. Care about the other person by remembering why you liked him or her in the first place. List your reasons why the breakup might be difficult for him or her, too. Finally, write down examples of the good times you had, and what those memories mean to you. It may take awhile, but someday you may even be friends again.

4

PRACTICE MENTAL AIKIDO

✳ The martial art of aikido is a seemingly gentle but extremely powerful and graceful method of self-defense. It offers amazing lessons in the art of resolving conflicts. Like the aikido artist, you can redirect negative energy aimed at you by learning not to overreact, yell or scream, or become bothered. Your weapons are your peace of mind and your lack of reaction. When you aren't rattled by conflicts, others will respect you, listen to you, and tend to see things your way.

Practice mental aikido on these theoretical situations, and then start using it in your real-life conflicts.

1. Your parents ask you who you're going out with. You usually don't like this and think they're prying, so your first reaction is often

_____.

Using mental aikido, you instead

_____.

2. Your best friend makes a negative comment about your clothes, hair, or other aspect of your appearance. Your response is generally

_____.

Using mental aikido, you instead

_____.

3. A teacher criticizes your response in class—something he or she has done in the past. When it happens, you usually

_____.

Using mental aikido, you instead

_____.

4. Your boyfriend/girlfriend is always late. You've expressed how much it bothers you, and now it really annoys you. Your typical reaction is

_____

Using mental aikido, you instead

_____

Now think of some real-life situations that you're sweating. Jot down some notes on how you might use mental aikido, rather than getting all fired up.

_____

_____

5

AVOID THE WORDS "I KNOW" WHEN SOMEONE IS TALKING

※ If you're in the habit of responding with "I know" when someone is talking to you, it doesn't really mean that you know it all. What it really means is that you're not listening very well to others. You're minimizing their comments, which can drive a deep wedge between you and the person you're talking to. Not only that, but saying "I know" can keep you from hearing important things. If you change the way you communicate by eliminating the "I knows" from your conversation, your relationships with people can improve greatly.

1. Who do you say "I know" to the most? Jot down the names. Be honest with yourself.
2. Why are you not listening to those people? Do you think there is nothing they can teach you? Do you really know everything there is to know? Write down your reason or reasons for each person on your list.
3. Now, accept that you may be missing out on a lot by not listening to each of these people, and that you may even be disrespecting them. Resolve to stop saying "I know" to each person, and practice this strategy every day with everyone you talk to.

6

CHECK OUT THESE ODDS!
(THE LIKELIHOOD THAT
EVERYONE WILL LIKE YOU)

❄ Everyone wants to be liked and accepted, but the odds are great that not *every* person you ever meet will like you. You can be nice to someone, but it doesn't mean that person will always be nice to you in return. Accept that, for whatever reason, there will always be someone who doesn't like you. It just means that this person isn't a perfect match for you. Your friends accept you for who you are, and those are the friends worth having. If you understand this, you won't feel as bad when you and a particular person don't click.

Not everyone you want to be friends with will end up being your friend. Be grateful for the good friends you have. Try the following.

1. Make a list of all your friends. This means really good friends who genuinely like you for who you are.
2. Next to each name, write what you like most about that person, or why you're especially glad that person is your friend.
3. Now, think for a moment of how different your life might be if that person wasn't your friend. Write what you would miss most about that person.
4. Think of a great compliment to pay each one of your friends. Tell them each something that shows them how much you appreciate their friendship. Write them down.
5. The next time you see each person, be sure to tell him or her how you feel about your friendship and how much it means to you.

7

GET OUT OF
THE EMERGENCY LANE

✳ Living life in the emergency lane means that you treat virtually everything as—you guessed it—an emergency! It's blowing life out of proportion, including everyday events and the smallest
small stuff. When you do that, life just isn't much fun. A lot of people are in this lane, but you don't have to be. There's no point in
becoming frustrated and upset about things over which you have no
control. Rather, accept what's happening and go with the flow.
When you make peace with the idea that life is never going to be
perfect, you can steer clear of the emergency lane.

Are you riding in the emergency lane? Read the three statements in each set below and find the one that best describes you and
how you react. Write the point value in the space beside the statement.

1. When I have too much homework, I

_____ always panic. I can't possibly finish it all. (1)

_____ sometimes panic. (2)

_____ never panic. I always get it done somehow. (3)

2. If I get stuck behind a slow driver, I

_____ sometimes get annoyed. (2)

_____ feel like I am in the worst possible situation. (1)

_____ know that we'll both eventually get to where we're going,
and I don't let it bother me. (3)

3. Some days my hair just won't do what I want it to, so I

_____ freak out if I can't get it to look right. (1)

_____ tie a bandanna around it and go on my way. (3)

_____ slow down, take a breath, and work with it. (2)

4. Picking up my kid sister from her school will make me late to meet the gang. I

_____ tell everyone that I'll be a bit late, pick her up, and go on my way. (3)

_____ argue about having to get her, but do it and give her the silent treatment. (2)

_____ get upset and yell about how I don't have any time for myself. (1)

SCORING

10–12: You take life in stride and move with the flow.

7–9: You should take a closer look at your emergencies and make them less significant.

4–6: You're definitely cruising in the emergency lane and need to find the exit!

8

BE OKAY WITH
YOUR BAD HAIR DAY

❋ A bad hair day is more about how we look and feel in general
than it is about hair. Understand that teens are pressured to
look like supermodels or popular celebrities. It's a cultural and adver-
tising trap, but you don't have to get stuck in it. Learn to let go of
your insecurities by deciding to like yourself just the way you are.
Making this decision will help you to feel better almost immediately.

The people who feel good about themselves and accept themselves as they are make healthy choices in life. They take care of
themselves without being obsessed with appearance. It's easy to
manage. Here are some suggestions.

1. Get at least eight hours of sleep a night.
2. Eat a good breakfast every morning (not just doughnuts).
3. Take a walk by yourself to enjoy the solitude and the natural sur-
   roundings.
4. Instead of TV on a sunny weekend afternoon, take a bike ride or
   go swimming.
5. Feeling edgy? Relax and do some yoga or stretching exercises.
6. Pass on the soda; drink water several times a day, instead.
7. Eat a healthy lunch, and hold the fries.
8. Be kind to your skin. Even teenagers need to wear sunscreen
   and avoid getting sunburned.
9. Skip the chips, and eat some fruit.
10. Get regular exercise, but remember that moderation is best.

9

DROP THE DRAMA

There's no question that a teenager's life can be filled with drama. On the other hand, making the decision to drop the drama, or at least some of it, can make life much happier and more peaceful.

How do you do that? By looking at life's dramas in a way that's better for your sanity and your happiness. Look at the following dramas and the scenarios for handling them. Which would make your life less stressful and happier in the long run?

After taking a test in school, you realize that you made a stupid mistake. So now you

1. beat yourself up all day long, playing the test over and over in your head. You're in a bad mood, you bark at everyone you talk to, and you don't concentrate on anything else that's going on in school that day.
2. remember that everyone makes mistakes, and that you'll use what you learned from this mistake to do better on your next test. Then you laugh at the mistake (it *was* pretty silly, after all), and go on with the rest of your day without dwelling on it.

At the last minute, your prom date gets sick and can't go. Of course you're disappointed. You

1. ask if you can help your sick friend; or you go alone; or you call friends who weren't going to the prom and make plans to do something with them.

2. get angry, hurt, sad, or upset and cause a scene. You make the person feel worse by dumping guilt on him or her.

Now, make a list of the current dramas in your life. For each one, write down how you are handling it. If you're making something too dramatic, write down how you can drop the drama.

10

GET HIGH!

Get naturally high—by learning to meditate. Tens of millions of people around the world use meditation on a daily basis to improve and enrich their lives. It makes you more peaceful, and contributes to clarity, happiness, and even productivity. If you try it and practice—ideally, every day—you'll find yourself getting along with people better, acting more loving, and definitely sweating the small stuff much less often.

Here's a simple breathing exercise to introduce you to meditation. Do this alone in a quiet place where you won't be disturbed.

1. Sit on the floor or on a chair that allows your feet to be flat on the floor.
2. Sit erect, keeping your head, neck, and back in a straight line.
3. Bring your full attention to your breathing. Breathe from your belly—it expands with each inhalation and recedes with each exhalation.
4. Sit and simply be aware of your breathing: in and out, in and out.
5. If your mind wanders, note what is distracting you, and then gently guide your attention back to your breathing. Do this every time your mind wanders, no matter how often, and don't be upset by the wandering.
6. Try this for five minutes, then ten, and work your way up to fifteen minutes. Be aware that what you're doing with this exercise is just being with your breathing.

Now that you've tried it, write about your experience.

- During the exercise, I felt

_____.

- My mind wandered to these things:

_____.

- Bringing my mind back to my breathing was easy/sort of easy/ difficult. (Circle one.)

- Being aware of my breathing made me think about

_____.

- After the exercise, I felt

_____.

11

TRY NOT TO BE A FAULTFINDER

One of the easiest things to do is to find fault, constantly pointing out the flaws and imperfections in yourself, others, society, and the world. It's almost guaranteed to make you unhappy, stressed out, and frustrated. When you look for problems and imperfections, that's what you'll see. Learn to allow things to be as they are most of the time. With practice, you'll get good at letting things go, even the things that really bug you. Life can be pretty awesome if you're not always finding fault with it.

Are you a faultfinder? Take this quiz and find out. Try to remember your answers the next time you feel compelled to find fault with something. For each answer, score 0 for *never*, 5 for *sometimes*, and 10 for *most of the time*.

_____ 1. Do you worry about what people think of your clothes, hair, or looks in general?

_____ 2. Do you point out things that are wrong with your prize-winning school project?

_____ 3. When people tell you about things they did, do you tell them how you would have done them better or differently?

_____ 4. Do you criticize your friends' behavior, dress, or looks?

_____ 5. Do you criticize your parents' or siblings' behavior, dress, or looks?

_____ 6. Are you always changing your hairstyle, makeup, or clothing style?

_____ 7. When you tell others about something wonderful that you've done, do you always have to include the little details that didn't go perfectly?

_____ 8. Do you always seek reassurance that things you've done are okay?

_____ 9. Do you tell people how they should handle situations, even if they never ask for your advice?

_____ 10. If someone makes a mistake while speaking, do you correct him or her out loud in front of other people?

_____ 11. Do you always complain about service in restaurants or stores?

_____ 12. Every time you go to a party, do you find something to complain about?

SCORING:

Less than 25: You're okay with the world.

25–50: You're pretty easygoing.

50–75: You might notice people avoiding you.

75–100: You're quite the critic.

More than 100: You're a faultfinder!

12

LET HIM HAVE HIS ACCIDENT
SOMEWHERE ELSE

To stop sweating the small stuff, you must learn to decide when to engage and when to ignore. In this day and age of road rage, it's important to learn to let angry, aggressive drivers pass you. Rather than escalate a dangerous situation, stay calm, pull over, and let the tailgating, headlight-flashing, horn-honking drivers go around you so they can have an accident elsewhere.

Do what you can to stay away from drivers with road rage. Figure out what the best choice is in each of the following situations.

1. You're getting onto the interstate and a driver apparently feels that you cut too abruptly in front of him. He lays on his horn, and you can see him shouting at you. You
   a. slow down a lot to punish him.
   b. move over into the next lane; then, as he passes you, you make a gesture at him.
   c. move to another lane or pull off the road, let him go, and then forget about him.

2. A driver is speeding and cutting wildly in and out of traffic. You
   a. get up behind her to get her license plate number so that you can call the cops.
   b. try to get in front of her so you can slow her down.
   c. put as much space between you and her as you can.

3. A driver seems to be angry about something you did, but you have no idea what. He pulls up beside you, rolls down the window, shouts, and shakes his fist. You:

a. speed up so you can get away from him.
b. turn your head toward him and stick your tongue out at him.
c. keep driving calmly without looking at him or making eye contact. If he persists in following you, you go somewhere you can get help.

(The correct answer in all cases is *c*.)

13

BE SELECTIVE WHEN CHOOSING YOUR BATTLES

Everyone has battles to fight in life. It's unavoidable. So the question becomes: Which battles do you choose to fight? Some people battle over practically anything. Living your whole life on a battleground is exhausting, and it makes people want to avoid you. It's better to be selective about your battles. When you choose your battles carefully, you'll often find that the ones you choose are much easier to win.

How do you choose the right battles? Try rating your battles from 1 (low importance) to 10 (high importance). Anything below a 5 is probably not worth doing battle for, so let it go, or resolve the issue without fighting to be right. A rating of 5 or 6 may even be questionable, but anything rated higher than 6 is worth your effort.

How would you rate the following potential conflicts? The suggested ratings are in parentheses after the statement.

_____ Friends disagree with you about what movie to see. (2)

_____ Parents give you a curfew time that you don't like. (5)

_____ A teacher wrongly accuses you of cheating on a quiz. (10)

_____ Your siblings use all the hot water before it's your turn in the shower. (5)

_____ A stranger cuts you off while driving. (1)

_____ A teammate makes a mistake that costs the team the game. (3)

_____ A sibling uses your car but never refills the gas tank. (7)

_____ Someone cuts in front of you in the grocery store check-out line. (1)

_____ Your parents mistakenly blame you for something your sibling did. (9)

Did your ratings come close to the suggestions? A good rule of thumb is this: When in doubt about how to rate a battle, assume that you're probably rating it too high. Keep your ratings low. Remember that some battles are worth fighting, but not many.

14

MAKE PEACE WITH
YOUR MISTAKES

✳ Life can be a series of mistakes—one right after another. We mess up, make amends, and change. We then go on with our lives, but sooner or later, we make other mistakes. Hopefully, we learn from them, make the necessary adjustments, and move on. Mistakes are inevitable and important. If you can see your mistakes as a means to becoming a better person, you'll get through difficult times more easily. Make peace with your mistakes, and learn what you can from them.

Below, make a list of mistakes that you've made recently. Go ahead, it's okay to admit that you've made them!

_____

_____

_____

_____

_____

For each mistake listed, what was your initial response to the mistake?

_____

_____

_____

_____

_____

For each mistake listed, write what you learned from the experience in one or two sentences.

_____

_____

_____

_____

_____

Any time that I make a mistake, here's what I do. Circle any responses from the list below that apply to you.

Get angry with myself.

Deny that I've made a mistake.

Become really frustrated.

Go on with life as if nothing happened.

Learn from what I did.

Remember what happened so I won't do it again.

Forgive myself.

Blame myself relentlessly.

Figure that I can't change things, so what?

Accept what I've done.

Try to blame someone else.

Decide that the world hates me.

If you circled any negative responses, see what you can do to change them to positive learning experiences. Write your ideas and thoughts here.

_____

_____

_____

_____

_____

15

BE HAPPY FOR OTHERS

✳ It's easy to get stuck in the envy habit, being a little jealous when someone you know is experiencing happiness or success. But if you can't feel genuinely happy for others when good things happen to them, it's really you who suffers. Wish others well and share in their happiness, then you get to experience their happiness with them. And when it's your turn to enjoy success, you'll get great joy from sharing your happiness with everyone else.

Do you have an "envy habit"? Take this quiz. Reflect on your answers, and see if you can break any envy habit you may have.

Event	I feel happy.	I feel envious.
1. A friend gets 100 on the big test.		
2. A sibling wins an essay contest.		
3. My best friend gets a new car for a birthday present.		
4. A friend's new boyfriend/ girlfriend is the greatest.		
5. A friend gets accepted to Harvard.		
6. My best friend's part-time job pays a lot of money.		

Event	I feel happy.	I feel envious.
7. A friend is going to Europe on vacation.		
8. A classmate has her poetry published in a magazine.		
9. A friend makes the first-string team.		
10. A close friend is valedictorian of the class.		
11. A friend gets to meet our favorite celebrity backstage.		
12. A sibling gets a standing ovation at the music recital.		
13. A friend gets picked for the school dance troupe.		
14. A friend's parents get a new boat.		
15. A friend is voted most likely to succeed by our class.		

If your answers reflect more envy than happiness, it's time for an attitude adjustment. Try to remember that everyone gets a chance to shine and that your time will come. In the meantime, work hard to reach your goals, and look forward to your friends' support.

16

VOLUNTEER YOUR TIME

Teens can and do make a difference—you have energy and enthusiasm, and a commitment to doing helpful things for others can go far. Volunteering your time for others or to a cause that you love helps you a lot, too. The gratification that you feel reduces stress and makes you happier. Teens often feel they lack control in their lives, that others are making all the decisions for them. When you help others, you realize that you can make a difference in people's lives. Your input can result in change. The decision is up to you. Volunteer with friends—you can spend time together having fun and being helpful to others. You'll all be helping to make your community a better place.

What can you do to help? Find something that interests you and donate your time to the cause. Here are some organizations where you might possibly do volunteer work; check off those you find interesting and then learn more about them.

_____ Hospitals (visit patients and deliver books, magazines, and treats)

_____ Children's charities (become a big brother/big sister)

_____ Elderly groups (visit nursing home residents or shut-ins)

_____ Hunger charities (work at soup kitchens or food banks)

_____ Literacy groups (read to kids or help others learn to read)

_____ "Adopt a child" through the mail (help poor children and families get necessities)

_____ Animal rescue charities (walk dogs, collect pet food donations, help families adopt pets)

_____ Environmental charities (help with community cleanup and awareness)

17

CHECK OUT THE SPACE
BETWEEN YOUR THOUGHTS

When you speak, there is a tiny pause between sentences, a space between your thoughts, that's often the key to taking the high road instead of the low. If you've ever been on the verge of making a decision or doing something but changed your mind at the last minute, you've experienced the space between your thoughts. In that moment of quiet, you saw the fork in the road—another option, an insight, a new direction. In those spaces lie clarity and wisdom from which you can benefit, especially when you're just not sure that the action you plan to take is the right one. Be open to what you can learn in those spaces.

Use the spaces between your thoughts to take the high road. In each instance below, fill in what you usually do, and then what you might do if you were open to the options the spaces show you. Remember your answers—and look for the spaces—if any of these come up in real life.

1. My parents criticize me. I usually

_____.

The spaces show me that instead I can

_____.

2. My kid brother/sister irritates me. I usually

_____.

The spaces show me that instead I can

_____ .

3. I didn't study for a quiz, but I can read the answers on my class-mate's paper next to me. I probably would

_____ .

The spaces show me that instead I can

_____ .

4. A kid at school tries to pick a fight with me, so I

_____ .

The spaces show me that instead I can

_____ .

18

ASK A TRUSTED FRIEND
OR FAMILY MEMBER,
"WHAT ARE MY WEAKNESSES?"

Your trusted friends and family members know you better than anyone else. They see you at your best and your worst, and they know your strengths and weaknesses. Because of this, they can help you see ways that you might change to improve your life. When you need help, don't be too proud, embarrassed, or defensive to ask their advice. But decide to listen to what's said, take the advice to heart, and learn from it. The rewards are potentially great if you're brave enough to try this strategy.

Who do you trust to ask for help, and how would you ask?

1. List trusted friends. Make sure these are people you can be comfortable with when asking for advice.
2. List family members you trust and are comfortable with.
3. What kind of advice are you seeking? Write it down.
4. List any specific questions you may want information about.

Remember you are the one asking for advice. You don't have to agree with what others tell you, but you must respect their opinions. In the end, you make the decisions, but getting advice from trusted loved ones can help you get there.

19

ROOT FOR THE UNDERDOG

It's easy to root for popular people—anyone can do that. The true measure of how kind you are as a human being is whether you can be nice to those who aren't popular, who may even be a little different. Embracing and accepting others shows that you can see beyond what's in at the moment. Doing so is a way of contributing to the world by making it a bit friendlier. Open your heart and widen your circle to include new friends. You'll set an example for others and feel good about yourself.

1. Do you know any underdogs? Make a list of people you know who aren't the most popular or trendy at the moment.
2. Can you support anyone on your list? Pick one and befriend that person. Write about your experience. Can you see how this experience helps you?
3. Were you ever an underdog? Think back, and recall any time when you felt like you weren't on top. Did anyone come to your rescue? How did they do it? Remember how grateful you were to that person and write about the whole experience.

20

MAKE PEACE
WITH BOREDOM

Most people can't stand being bored, even for a moment. Something has to be going on, turned on, or being planned. Being constantly stimulated actually sets you up for boredom—your mind keeps looking for more and more. When this happens, inner creativity disappears and is replaced by outer activities. It's okay if something isn't going on all the time; you can learn to sit still with nothing happening. Do that for a few minutes at a time, and you'll become a happier person who gets more joy from the things you already spend time doing.

You can make peace with boredom by not trying so hard to be busy. Take this quiz to see if you can allow yourself to be bored. Read the statements, and then select the one that best describes you. Write the point value in the space beside the statement.

1. While waiting for the school bus, I might

_____ finish the homework that I didn't do the night before. (1)

_____ relax and look at the trees, the birds, and the sunshine. (3)

_____ start reading a book. (2)

2. If I have some extra time before class, I

_____ go over the material for the class. (2)

_____ try to grab a snack, meet friends, and finish homework for later in the day. (1)

_____ close my eyes for a moment and try to clear my mind. (3)

3. I've finished cleaning up my room, and it went more quickly than I thought. I

_____ tidy up a bit more. (2)

_____ look frantically for something to do—I have an hour to kill before I go to the dentist. (1)

_____ sit quietly and think about nothing for a while. (3)

4. My friend cancels out on our movie date at the last minute. I

_____ go by myself. (2)

_____ quickly call all my other friends to see if there's something else to do. (1)

_____ take a bubble bath. (3)

5. My softball game is canceled due to rain. I

_____ go home and watch sports on TV. (2)

_____ stop at the Y to see if there's a crowd hanging out or playing basketball. (1)

_____ go home, sit in a comfy chair, and watch the rain. (3)

SCORING:

5–8: You can't be bored and must always be doing something. You should slow down and relax a bit.

9–12: You can relax sometimes but have a tendency to try to keep busy.

13–15: You make peace with boredom and allow yourself to be bored.

21

DON'T LET YOUR LOW MOODS TRICK YOU

* Moods can be powerful and deceptive. When your mood is good, you feel confident, responsible, happy, and secure—in short, you enjoy life. Everybody is a cool person, and you feel there's no problem you can't solve. But when your mood is low, everything turns around—you feel insecure, depressed, angry, stressed out, and perhaps even frightened. You take things personally, don't like yourself or others very much, and probably sweat the small stuff a lot. At times like these, try to remember that your life hasn't changed, only your mood has, which makes things seem worse than they really are.

Are you sometimes fooled by your moods? Answer the following questions.

1. Do you think you're moody? Have your parents, other family members, or friends ever told you you're moody?

2. How do you feel when you're in a bad mood? Check any that apply. Add any feelings that aren't listed.

_____ Angry

_____ Irritable

_____ Critical

_____ Snippy

_____ Sarcastic

_____ Unhappy

_____ Indecisive

_____ Impatient

_____ Grumpy

3. How do others react to your bad moods? Do you get defensive if they tell you that you're in "one of your moods"?

4. How do you usually express your bad moods?

5. What puts you in a bad mood? List as many things as you can think of.

_____

_____

_____

6. What makes you happy? List the things that can turn your bad mood around.

_____

_____

_____

7. Write about a time when you did something during a bad mood that you regretted.

_____

_____

_____

8. How would you handle that situation now that you know your moods can deceive you?

_____

_____

_____

22

DON'T LET THE LOW MOODS OF OTHERS TRICK YOU, EITHER

* Everyone has low moods, including friends, teachers, siblings, parents, neighbors, and strangers. Like you, they'll be more negative and pessimistic during their low moods. They may be critical, defensive, and do and say mean things. Low moods trick all of us. Recognize the deceptive power of moods, and you'll take them less personally. Then you can see what's really going on when others aren't acting like themselves.

Can you look beyond the behavior of others, recognize that they're having a low mood, and not take it personally? For each behavior below, fill in how you (a) could see the behavior in the worst possible way, and (b) might look beyond it to see what's really going on.

1. Your best friend always remembers your birthday . . . until this year.

   a. _____

   b. _____

2. You're in your room studying, working hard to solve a problem in your head. Your mom walks by your room and exclaims, "Why are you just sitting around daydreaming when you've got work to do?"

   a. _____

   b. _____

3. Your favorite TV show is on and your sibling is talking loudly on the phone. You ask if he could please go to another room, and he shouts, "*You* go to another room, twerp!"

a. _____

b. _____

4. Your friend's last haircut was a disaster, and the two of you usually kid about the hack job. Today, you get snapped at.

a. _____

b. _____

Can you recall a time when a friend treated you poorly? Do you think that behavior could be attributed to a bad mood? How would you react or feel differently the next time it happens?

_____

_____

_____

_____

23

SEE YOUR CHOICES AS
FORKS IN THE ROAD

Look back a few years, and you'll see that the major choices you made were like forks in the road—each decision or choice led you in a certain direction. A different choice would probably have taken you elsewhere. Learning to view your choices as forks in the road can be very empowering and reassuring. You can take charge of your life and know that it's never too late to change your direction.

Learn to see what might happen depending on which choice you make. In each of the following scenarios, write what might happen if you choose one fork in the road, and then what might happen if you choose the other.

1. Everyone's teasing a kid at school.

   If I stand up for that kid,

   _____.

   If I join the teasing,

   _____.

2. There's a big party at my friend's house, but I have to study for a huge science test.

   If I go to the party,

   _____.

If I stay home and study,

_____.

3. My friends are all going to a party where alcohol is going to be served.

   If I go with them,

   _____.

   If I decline to go,

   _____.

4. My parents say I'm never home anymore. They want to have an evening alone with me.

   If I stay home with them,

   _____.

   If I say no and go out with my friends,

   _____.

5. Someone offers me drugs or a cigarette. Everyone else is trying it.

   If I try it,

   _____.

   If I say "No thanks" and walk away,

   _____.

Have you recently faced making a decision that seemed like a fork in the road? Write about it. Which fork did you choose and why? What might have happened if you had chosen the other fork in the road? Are you glad you made the choice that you did? If not, why?

_____

_____

_____

_____

_____

24

GET INVOLVED IN SPORTS

❋ Sports can be therapeutic, satisfying, and a great boon to your mental and physical health. Deciding to participate in sports can be a life-enhancing decision that brings you pleasure for the rest of your life. There is a sport to suit every individual's need, whether you are a team player or more of an individual, naturally talented or professionally taught. Regardless of winning and losing, playing sports can help you to stop sweating the small stuff and let you take out frustrations by expending physical energy. You don't have to be good at it—just taking part makes you a winner!

Have you tried participating in sports? Perhaps you never thought you could. This true/false quiz can help you to see if you have any misconceptions about sports and your ability to play.

1. Only guys can play sports.   T   F

2. You have to be really strong to play sports.   T   F

3. No one would want me on a team because
   I'm not athletic.   T   F

4. You need good coordination to play sports.   T   F

5. If you're not out to win, the kids don't want you
   on their team.   T   F

6. I'm too out of shape to get involved in any sports. T   F

Here's a list of some of the benefits that being involved in sports can bring. Put a check beside the things that you would like to accomplish. See if you can motivate yourself to begin an athletic program of your own.

_____ Gain better cardiovascular fitness

_____ Gain better overall physical fitness

_____ Strengthen muscles

_____ Become agile and limber

_____ Horse around with friends/teammates

_____ Meet new friends

_____ Improve coordination

_____ Enjoy healthy competition

_____ Learn cooperation and teamwork

_____ Practice good sportsmanship

_____ Always have something to do

_____ Build character

_____ Expend physical energy

25

BECOME A
TEENAGE WARRIOR

Life is full of difficulties, but you don't have to let them ruin you, turn you sour and apathetic, or destroy your spirit. If you look at them the right way, life's difficulties can be a source of growth, wisdom, perspective, and patience. Don Juan said, "The difference between an ordinary man and a warrior is that a warrior takes everything as a challenge, while an ordinary man takes everything as a blessing or a curse." Become a teenage warrior by looking at your problems differently. Find the hidden gift in every hurdle. When something goes wrong, see what you can learn from it.

You can become a teenage warrior if you're ready! Try the following steps.

- Who do you respect? List your heroes, including people you actually know. Note why you respect each one, and how each person approached his or her challenges.
- List people you know or have heard of who constantly complain about everything. How do these people respond to their challenges?
- Look at the two lists and note the differences in how the people on each handle difficulties.
- You can be like your heroes! List some of your recent problems and how you handled them. Instead of being troubled and feeling bad about them, see if you can find something positive or a lesson to be learned from each one. Write them down.

Look at your problems in this new light, and learn to respond to challenges. This will enable you to become a teenage warrior!

26

PUT IT ON PAPER

✳ There's tremendous value in putting your thoughts on paper. The act of writing, even typing on a computer, is a harmless way to sort through, ponder, reflect upon, and express your emotions. It can relieve a burden that you may be carrying and help you to let go of negative feelings. Healing can begin once things are "off your chest." Plus, if you write down your positive feelings, you can reinforce how much you have to be grateful for in your life.

Put it on paper now! Try these exercises.

- Write a short letter to someone you know and focus on something positive. Tell the person—friend, relative, neighbor, teacher—how grateful you are for something in your life. You don't have to mail the letter, but you never know, you might want to.
- Has someone made you angry recently? Write that person a short letter and tell him or her what you think. You're not going to mail this one, so really cut loose. Afterward, see if you don't feel much better, then tear up the letter.
- Get your bad feelings off your chest. Write down any negative thoughts and feelings that you're having right now. After you do that, see if you can turn the negative thoughts into positive ones. For example, "I played lousy at the basketball game and the team hates me." Turn that thought into: "I know the team doesn't really hate me. I did the best I could that day; I'll do better next time."
- Get your positive feelings on the page. Write down some things you're grateful for in your life, no matter how big or

small. For example, "I'm grateful that I live near the ocean, because I love watching the sun set over the water." You may quickly realize how much you can truly appreciate the simple things in life.

- What else are you grateful for? There's no time like now to make a list. Refer back to this list any time you feel things aren't going well in your life.

27

DON'T EXPECT LIFE TO BE
EASY OR TROUBLE-FREE

✱ You can learn to be more accepting of the way things are in life rather than insisting that things be different or better. We expect life to go a certain way. If it goes as we've planned, we're okay. If not, we often lose it and sweat a lot of small stuff. Life comes with hassle, frustration, and difficulty, and no one is exempt from it. Accepting this fact can make life seem a bit easier and more trouble-free.

Are you flexible in life? Learning to be flexible can make you more relaxed. When you don't expect life to be perfect, going with the flow is much easier. In the following situations, what might you do when faced with a similar situation in reality? What might you do to become more flexible?

1. You've just started working on a school project when your parents need you to help them with something right away.

   You would

   _____.

   To be more flexible, you would

   _____.

2. You're ready to go on vacation, but your kid brother/sister becomes ill.

   You would

   _____.

To be more flexible, you would

_____ .

3. You're going on your first date with someone you've admired for a while. At the last minute your date calls and cancels.

You would

_____ .

To be more flexible, you would

_____ .

4. You have plans to attend a certain college, but you aren't accepted.

You would

_____ .

To be more flexible, you would

_____ .

5. You're ready to go to the big game, but your neighbor is seriously in need of help, and there's no one else around.

You would

_____ .

To be more flexible, you would

_____ .

6. Your boyfriend/girlfriend is sick and can't go with you to the big year-end dance.

   You would

   _____ .

   To be more flexible, you would

   _____ .

7. You thought you would get along well with everyone on your debate team, but there's friction among the members.

   You would

   _____ .

   To be more flexible, you would

   _____ .

28

DARE TO SHOW ENTHUSIASM

❋ Enthusiasm is a spark of energy, a sense of interest and inspiration that ignites effort, creativity, and hard work. It's almost impossible to succeed without enthusiasm. It's that important. Enthusiasm can move you through life's difficulties and sweeten your victories. The successful people you admire all have enthusiasm in common. You can join them by daring to adjust your attitude and being sincere about anything you do.

Have you been less than enthusiastic about certain things in your life lately? See if you can dare to show enthusiasm in the future. Check off the areas below where you didn't show much enthusiasm. Then note how you might approach these things differently next time.

_____ Baby-sitting

_____

_____ Cleaning your room

_____

_____ Washing the car

_____

_____ School projects

_____

_____ Music lessons

_____

_____ Helping parents

_____

_____ Household chores

_____

_____ Team practice

_____

_____ Visiting relatives

_____

_____ Art projects

_____

_____ Health and fitness

_____

_____ Learning new things

_____

_____ Meeting new people

_____

_____ Going places with family

_____

_____ Helping siblings

_____

_____ Dating

_____

_____ Making new friends

_____

_____ Writing thank-you notes

_____

_____ Volunteering your time

_____

29

FIND PEACE THROUGH GIVING

There's nothing quite like the feeling of knowing you've done something really nice for someone, whether the person acknowledges it or even knows that you've done it. If you think about what makes you feel good, you'll probably agree that giving to others is at or near the top of your list. Giving doesn't have to be a major production—doing small things with great love can really help to change the world. Giving doesn't have to be material. It can be an act of kindness or sharing. By becoming more giving, you'll become a much happier and more peaceful person.

How many ways can you think of to give to others? Here are some suggestions. Add your own ideas to the list. Now, pick an item from the list and do it. Then pick another, and get into the habit of giving.

_____ Donate money to charity

_____ Donate used clothing, books, or toys to charity

_____ Baby-sit for a harried parent

_____ Take a meal to an elderly shut-in

_____ Pick up litter along your street

_____ Teach a kid how to shoot hoops

_____ Help paint homes for those in need

_____ Serve holiday meals at a food bank

_____ Feed animals at the local shelter

_____ Help adults learn computers

_____ Become a "foster grandchild"

_____ Volunteer for community service

_____ Help disaster relief in time of need

_____ Take an elderly person shopping

_____ Become a big brother/big sister

_____ Spearhead a class charity effort

What other ways can you think of to give, even in the smallest ways? Add them to the list.

30

BECOME 25 PERCENT
LESS CRITICAL

Virtually anyone can become 25 percent less critical if they set their mind to it. As you become less critical, you'll experience a corresponding increase in your own level of satisfaction. You'll also find yourself being more open-minded, and your learning curve will sharpen. And get this: Others will find you more fun to be around, too!

You can back off on criticizing others and turn being critical into something more productive. Go through these exercises and learn how.

1. Your best friend has a habit of snapping chewing gum and it annoys you. Your critical response might be

_____.

Instead, you say

_____.

2. Your parents love a certain TV show, but you think it's sappy. They can't wait to watch it each week. Your critical response might be

_____.

Instead, you say

_____.

3. A friend has undergone a complete makeover. You really don't like the new look—you didn't think there was anything wrong with the old one. Your critical response might be

_____.

Instead, you say

_____.

4. Your new boyfriend/girlfriend likes a completely different type of music than you. Actually, you can't stand listening to what he/she likes. Your critical response might be

_____.

Instead, you say

_____.

5. At a gathering after practice, the talk among your teammates turns to bad-mouthing the coach. Last season you jumped right in and criticized by saying

_____.

But this season, you say

_____.

Where else can you cut down on being critical? List some things you know you criticize people for. Write down what you could say instead.

3 1

WALK AWAY

✱ Walking away from conflict isn't being weak. It takes a strong, wise person to walk away from physical conflict, as well as verbal arguments that can lead to stress, heartache, anxiety, or hassle. In most conflicts, you have a choice of battling to prove that you're right or simply walking away. Sometimes you must fight back, but it's not as often as you might think. It's usually wiser and more practical to turn your back on the argument, thus saving yourself more grief, hassle, and aggravation than you can possibly imagine.

What would you do in the following situations—fight back (F) or walk away (W)? Think about your answers and why you chose the answer you did.

1. Someone calls you a name in front of your friends. F   W

2. Someone tailgates you on the freeway. F   W

3. A classmate accuses you of cheating on a quiz, but you didn't. F   W

4. You give a speech in class, and a student corrects one of your facts. F   W

5. Some big kids are relentlessly picking on your younger sibling. F   W

6. You're in a disagreement, and the other person absolutely has to have the last word. F   W

7. Someone tries to slap you during an argument. F   W

8. Someone cuts in line in front of you at the movies. F   W

9. Someone accuses you of stealing something in a
   store, but you didn't.   F   W

10. Your parents accuse you of something that you
    didn't do and try to ground you.   F   W

Have you walked away from potential fights? List them. How did you feel walking away? Strong? Weak?

_____

_____

_____

Did you ever get into a fight that you wish you had walked away from? Write about it. How would you have handled it today?

_____

_____

_____

32

ALLOW A NEW IDEA TO
COME TO YOU

✱ Our inner wisdom often gets lost in the crowd of thoughts, ideas, plans, and fears that run through our minds. Trying to find solutions to our problems can often cause us to feel trapped and even more frustrated. It's best to relax your mind, let your thoughts go, and allow yourself to be calm. Tell yourself that you need a smart, appropriate answer to your problem, issue, or dilemma. Clear your mind and let go of your thoughts. You may be surprised to find that your best ideas will come to you without you actively thinking, struggling, or forcing the issue. Sometimes just sleeping on a problem can help. The answers are already in there, just give them a chance to surface!

You can create an environment that encourages the flow of new ideas by learning to quiet your mind. Here are some suggestions.

1. Sit quietly, take a deep breath, close your eyes, and think about a beautiful place. It can be a real place that you found peaceful and soothing, or a place that exists only in your imagination. With your eyes closed, visualize this soothing place. Describe it on paper.

2. Now engage all your senses in this special place. Take a breath: What do you smell? Listen carefully: What sounds do you hear? Now picture yourself in this place. How do you look? What are you doing? This is like a vacation list for your mind—you can visit these places whenever you want to quiet your mind.

3. Any time you need guidance, inspiration, solutions to problems, or new ideas, visit a place where you can calm your mind. Do you have a list of problems or little troubles to sort out? Write them down. Then, one by one, over a period of time, go to your quiet place and allow new thoughts and ideas to come to you.

33

GET READY EARLY

✳ Being in a hurry is stressful—you're rushing around, worrying about how busy you are. Teenagers today are often stretched for time. They are highly scheduled and often pushed to their physical and mental limits. Rushing, however, is a stress that can easily be eliminated. All it takes is your willingness to see that the problem lies within. (This is a plus because it means you have the ability to control and change things!) It's not a lack of time that's the problem, it's that you don't give yourself quite enough time. Make a commitment to get ready early, whether it's in the morning before school or at the beginning of a big book report. Getting an early start makes the process more peaceful and enjoyable and keeps you from sweating the small stuff.

Are you a "deadline junkie"? Do you always wait until the last minute to do things? This true/false exercise will help you see if you need to commit to getting an earlier start on things.

1. I know I do my best work under pressure.   T   F

2. I tend to underestimate how long it will take me to do things.   T   F

3. When I start a project, I somehow always end up pushing hard at the end.   T   F

4. I find myself staying up late and getting up early to work on things.   T   F

5. During a project, I get very stressed and don't have time for anything but the work.   T   F

6. If I have an appointment, I fiddle around at home until the last minute.　　　T　　F

7. It almost always happens: On the way to an appointment, I get stuck in a big traffic jam.　　　T　　F

8. I'm always so tired that I want to sleep as long as I possibly can.　　　T　　F

9. I let projects and chores pile up until I can't possibly finish them all in time.　　　T　　F

10. I'm always running around the house looking for something when it's time to go.　　　T　　F

11. I often rush out of the house and forget things.　　　T　　F

12. I usually end up cramming for exams.　　　T　　F

13. When I'm on my way out, a distraction like the phone always makes me late.　　　T　　F

14. I never seem to have enough time.　　　T　　F

15. I'm always too busy.　　　T　　F

34

AVOID THE NINETY/TEN TRAP

Most of us tend to focus our attention on the negative. Maybe 10 percent of our lives isn't going well. Yet 90 percent of what happens during the day is usually pretty good. Focusing on what's wrong with life instead of what is generally okay is the basis of the 90/10 trap. Every day is different, and some days are truly bad, but it typically plays out that the majority of the time is good. Be aware of a tendency to focus on the negative and try to turn it around to emphasize the positive. When you are aware of what's going right in your life you can deal with hassles more easily.

There are a lot of things going right in your life! Take a moment to look at the 90 percent of your day that was positive and gain some insight about the rest of your day.

1. Write in detail about:
   - the best thing that happened to you today
   - the most pleasant experience that you had in dealing with another person today
   - the best food that you ate all day
   - the most fun that you had all day
   - the most interesting thing that happened
   - the most interesting person you met
   - the most beautiful thing you saw in nature
   - the most beautiful song you heard
   - the most peaceful and relaxed moment you had during the day

2. Ask your friends to tell you about the best parts of their day. Does listening to these make you see more positive things in your day? Why or why not? Write about it.

3. You experienced different emotions today. Write about:
   - how you felt most of the day
   - how many times you were happy and feeling up
   - how many times you were sad or angry and feeling down

Are you focusing on the bad feelings? See if you can change your focus to the good feelings.

35

BE THE ROLE MODEL

There's no question that having role models is important. It's equally important to *be* a good role model. Don't leave it up to celebrities or other adults who can fall short. Become a person others look up to right now. Role models set great examples for others in areas of kindness, morality, generosity, caring, patience, thoughtfulness, and dedication, to name a few. Anyone can be a role model if he or she decides that it's important. You can positively affect people by your own behavior. The decisions you make and the way you conduct yourself can make you feel good about yourself, too.

What makes a good role model? Consider these things.

1. Who do you consider to be your role models? What traits do these people have? Why do you think these traits are admirable? Write about them.
2. Do you share any traits with these people? List them.
3. How might a teen be a good role model to a younger person? Look at this list of traits and put a check beside any traits that you have.

_____ Is kind to others

_____ Tries hard in school

_____ Is a nice person

_____ Is ethical

_____ Is always willing to help

_____ Is truthful

_____ Doesn't cut classes

_____ Gets involved at school

_____ Doesn't cheat

_____ Has a sense of fairness

_____ Handles stress well

_____ Listens well

_____ Truly cares about others

_____ Is generous

_____ Has patience

Can you think of other traits that a good role model might have?
Add them to the list.

36

DON'T UNDERESTIMATE
YOURSELF

Many of us inadvertently create stress in our lives by making the mistake of underestimating ourselves. If we fail to have adequate confidence in our abilities, intuition, and wisdom, we must rely on others to guide and direct us. For teens, especially, this can encourage us to seek acceptance and approval from others. But if we give ourselves the credit we deserve and have confidence in ourselves, we have control over our feelings, and we won't find ourselves vulnerable to the opinions of others.

Confidence is contagious. If you believe in yourself, others will, too. How self-confident are you? Take this quiz and find out. Select the answer that best describes you for each item, and write the point value in the space before the statement.

1. The big sports game is coming up, and the coach is relying on you to lead the team to victory. You've done it before, but can you do it again? You feel

_____ panicky—the pressure is too much. (1)

_____ edgy, but ready to go and give it your best. (2)

_____ good and strong—you've beat this team before, and you can do it again. (3)

2. A friend of your parents has offered you a great summer job. It won't be easy, so you

_____ are worried that you'll let your parents down. (1)

_____ feel challenged, but you can't pass up this great opportunity. (2)

_____ are anxious to get started—you know you'll learn as you go. (3)

3. You're visiting an older cousin in another state, and you're invited to a party with some of his or her friends. You feel

_____ a bit shy, but you've been in situations before where you didn't know anybody at all. (2)

_____ good about yourself and ready to get out and make even more new friends. (3)

_____ like a shrinking violet—you beg off so that you don't have to face so many strangers. (1)

4. You just got new glasses. You've seen other kids who have glasses being made fun of, and you

_____ aren't concerned—you've picked the coolest frames from the latest styles. (3)

_____ hope the bullies don't make too much fun of you. (2)

_____ know you're absolutely going to die when someone makes the first remark. (1)

5. You're given a complicated project at school. This counts for a big part of your grade in this particular class. You feel

_____ unsure that you can figure out how to complete the project. (2)

_____ really worried that you'll blow your entire grade. (1)

_____ unclear about how you'll do the project, but certain that you'll find a way and get it done. (3)

SCORING:

3–6: You lack self-confidence and probably underestimate yourself most of the time. Remind yourself regularly that you're a competent person who can rise to any occasion.

7–11: You may underestimate yourself a little, but you're still fairly confident.

12–15: You're self-confident, and you don't underestimate yourself.

37

GET OVER
COMPLETION ANXIETY

❋ Have you ever worked long and hard on a project, only to abandon it near the very end? For some reason, finishing things can make some people anxious or uncomfortable. This is known as "completion anxiety," and it can create an enormous amount of stress for a teen. Your life as a young adult is often about jumping hurdles and reaching goals. Completion anxiety may be the result of resentment at all you have to do and be. But leaving things unfinished only burdens you even more and can cause others to become disappointed with you. It is human nature for people to notice what we haven't done instead of what we have done. To reduce the stress, make an effort to finish things—all the way, 100 percent—whenever it's within your power to do so. Without things hanging over your head, you'll eliminate stress, accomplish your goals, and prepare for your future.

What's on your list of not-quite-finished things? See if you have completion anxiety.

1. At school, I started

   a. _____

   b. _____

   c. _____

   I finished _____.

   I didn't finish _____.

The reasons why I didn't finish the above are

_____ .

2. At home, I started

a. _____

b. _____

c. _____

I finished . _____ .

I didn't finish _____ .

The reasons why I didn't finish the above are

_____ .

3. Other things that I've started are

a. _____

b. _____

c. _____

I finished _____ .

I didn't finish _____ .

The reasons why I didn't finish the above are

_____ .

Can you now finish or resolve any of the above unfinished tasks, chores, or problems? Try to do at least one this week. Do as many as you feel comfortable doing. After you finish each one, fill in the following.

- After I finished, I felt

_____.

- I think the payoff for not finishing was

_____.

- I overcame that by

_____.

- To prevent leaving things undone in the future, I plan to

_____.

38

SEE THE POSSIBILITIES

❋ Teens are often self-defeating. They may give up on something without trying, perhaps caught up in their frustration and the drama of any given situation. One of the secrets to staying calm and happy is to remain hopeful. And without question, one of the best ways to remain hopeful is to see the possibilities. When we become absorbed in the difficulties we face, we lose our perspective and our optimism is overshadowed by fear. We forget that we've overcome obstacles before and that we're really quite resilient.

You can see the possibilities—of meeting a challenge, winning, achieving a goal, or overcoming a problem—by remembering how many times you've done it before. Go through these exercises to help you see the possibilities in any difficulties that you may currently be facing.

1. Are you facing some challenges right now? List them.
2. Think back. Have you gone through similar situations before? For each item above, write about a time in the past when you dealt with the same or a similar problem. How did you handle each problem before?
3. What was the outcome each time? If it wasn't necessarily good, what did you learn from it that you might use now to avoid another negative outcome?

39

PRACTICE NOT SWEATING THE
REALLY SMALL STUFF

✳ Very few of us learn, at an early enough age, to not sweat the small stuff. As a result, most of us lack the perspective, patience, and cool required to live a happy life with a minimal amount of stress. To get this perspective, start with the really small stuff and build on your success. Practice reacting differently to the small stuff that happens in your life. You'll start to accept that there will always be things in life that are less than ideal or irritating. Pretty soon, things that used to bother you won't bother you anymore, and you'll begin to put many more things into the category of "It's not worth sweating over."

Name some things that irritate you but are really small and relatively insignificant. (For example, your brother or sister constantly walks into your room without knocking.)

_____

_____

_____

For each irritating thing that you named, write down what your typical reaction to it is. (In the above example, say that you always get angry and agitated, and scream at your sibling to please knock first.)

_____

_____

Now, write down a new and different reaction that you can practice, one that is more patient and not annoyed. (For example, do something funny when the above situation arises by taking your sibling by the hand, leading him or her out of the room, closing the door, and demonstrating how to knock before entering.)

_____

_____

_____

Make a commitment to practice these new, less reactive ways of dealing with your irritations. This is how you practice not sweating the really small stuff!

40

DON'T KEEP YOUR PAIN
A SECRET

Being in emotional pain is hard enough, don't compound it by keeping the pain all to yourself. Rather than turn inward, as many teens do, learn to reach out to others. This can make you feel empowered and help you heal more quickly and completely. Being with others when you're suffering is often comforting and nourishing, as people are an important source of support and strength. If you think you would be a burden to friends or family by reaching out, remind yourself of how readily you make yourself available to the people you care about. Allow yourself that same comfort.

Who can you reach out to? Put a check in front of each person who represents someone to whom you might turn if you had problems. Write the person's name in the following space. When you're having problems and feel like you could use some help, don't keep your pain a secret. Turn to this list, and find someone to share your troubles with.

_____ Mother   _____

_____ Father   _____

_____ Teacher   _____

_____ Coach   _____

_____ Sibling   _____

_____ Close friend   _____

_____ Doctor   _____

_____ Relative   _____

_____ Clergy person   _____

_____ Boss   _____

_____ School counselor   _____

_____ Family friend   _____

_____ Teammate   _____

41

MAKE A GOOD

FIRST IMPRESSION

❋ Like it or not, first impressions are very important, because once an opinion is formed about you, it's tough to change it. A bad first impression can follow you like a shadow, but so will a good first impression. If you give off a positive, friendly, upbeat image to the people you meet, that image feeds on itself and often leads to great experiences.

If there are people who act negatively toward you, think back to the first impression you gave them, and see if that may have influenced them. In fact, look closely at your first impressions. How do you present yourself to people? Are there things you can change? Here is a checklist of things that help make a good first impression. Look at the list for ideas, and use whatever you can to improve your first impression.

_____ A friendly attitude (extend a hand first; introduce yourself; have an open, inviting manner)

_____ A pleasant facial expression (smile; project warmth and sincerity; make eye contact)

_____ Good manners (address older people by the appropriate title, such as Mr. or Miss; use polite words; be respectful to others; don't interrupt when others are talking)

_____ A pleasant speaking manner (speak clearly and confidently; look at the person to whom you're speaking; avoid sarcasm, puns, and inside jokes; curb use of slang)

_____ Proper physical appearance (be clean; keep clothing neat; care for your skin and hair; have good posture and carriage)

Are there other ways to make a good impression? Think about it, and jot down any ideas that you might come up with.

42

BE CAREFUL TO AVOID THE "I'LL SHOW YOU" TRAP

✳ It's tempting to lash out and prove a point when you get angry with your parents. But if you get caught in the "I'll show you" trap, it's really *you* who suffers. What you choose to do or not do may elate or disappoint your parents, so you must always be careful to avoid self-destructive choices that deny you something you truly love. Take a step back and avoid this trap. You'll get a lot of satisfaction from knowing you're too strong to fall for it.

Have you ever been caught in the "I'll show you" trap? List the times you took action specifically to upset your parents. For each one, answer the following questions.

1. Why were you angry with your parents?
2. What did you do to show them?
3. How did they react?
4. How did you feel when they reacted the way they did?
5. Be honest: Did it hurt you more than it hurt them? Write about how you felt because of it.

43

EXPERIENCE PERFECT
IMPERFECTION

Often, an overwhelming source of stress for teens is the perceived need for perfection. Perfectionism and happiness don't mix, whether you expect perfection in yourself or in others. It's true that you want to be and do your best, but not being satisfied with who you are or your accomplishments is a recipe for frustration. Likewise, expecting others to live up to perfection is a recipe for disaster. Rather than focus on your—or others'—shortcomings, failures, and deficiencies, make a conscious decision to let go of the need for perfection. As you do, you'll realize that in most cases, things are already perfect in their own way, and that you can find perfection in life's imperfections.

Are you hung up on being perfect? Find out with this quiz. Remember your answers the next time you catch yourself focusing on shortcomings and failures, whether your own or someone else's.

1. Do you spend a lot of time getting ready for school in the morning, making sure your hair, clothes, and/or makeup are perfect?
   Yes   No

2. Do you constantly second-guess your own choices of clothing and hairstyles?   Yes   No

3. Do you constantly think about the things you didn't get done each day?   Yes   No

4. If you get a B on a quiz, do you feel frustrated that you didn't get an A?   Yes   No

5. Do you look in the mirror and make mental note of the physical faults you perceive?   Yes   No

6. Do you beat up on yourself for forgetting things or making little mistakes?   Yes   No

7. Do you buy clothes but not like them by the time you get them home?   Yes   No

8. Are you constantly fixing things in your room, around the house, or at school?   Yes   No

If you've answered yes to more than three of these questions, you're looking for perfection in yourself. You would do well to learn to accept yourself and your life as they are.

44

DARE TO BE ETHICAL

Being ethical is doing the right thing. It means that you're interested in what's honest and right, not just what's best for you. Something almost magical happens to your spirits when you know in your heart that you're an honest, ethical person, no matter what.

Dare to be ethical in the following situations. What would you do?

1. A clerk in the supermarket gives you a ten-dollar bill for change instead of a one-dollar bill. You
   a. take the money and run—it was her mistake.
   b. tell her she made a mistake, and get the correct change.
   c. tell her boss that she's a lousy cashier.

2. The night before your book report's due, you still haven't started writing. You learn that your older brother did a report on the same book for a different teacher five years ago. He got an A, and he gives you a copy of the report. You
   a. congratulate your brother on getting such a good grade.
   b. put your brother's report away, roll up your sleeves, and get down to writing your own report.
   c. retype your brother's report, changing a word or two, and turn it in as your own.

3. You accidentally scrape the bumper of your neighbor's car as you turn your dad's car into your driveway. No one sees you because it's late (your basketball game went into overtime). You
   a. get some touch-up paint from the garage and try to fix both cars while no one's looking.

b. tell your parents, and then tell the neighbor (even if you have to wait until morning).

c. sneak into the house, jump in bed, and don't tell anyone—ever.

4. Someone has written something nasty on the blackboard in history class before the teacher gets to the room; now she's upset, but she blames a student you know didn't do it and sends the wrong teen to see the principal. You

a. take the blame yourself.

b. talk to the kid who really did it and tell him that he should confess.

c. keep your mouth shut and mind your own business.

5. A neighborhood child is constantly being teased by others because she wears thick glasses. The teasing hurts her feelings and she thinks no one likes her. One day you see several kids teasing her. You

a. join the fun.

b. keep heading home—your favorite TV show starts in five minutes.

c. stand up for the kid—explain to the others that no one likes having his or her feelings hurt. (They'll listen to you, because you're the bigger kid.)

If you have questions about what the "right" answers to these questions are, then spend some time putting yourself in others' shoes. How would you want to be treated in these situations if you stood to gain or suffer from the consequences? Being ethical means being thoughtful—and that is something both teens and adults should strive for.

45

BECOME BUTTON-PROOF

There will always be people who push your buttons, who do things that annoy or upset you. Sometimes they do it by accident, but some people do it on purpose. Strive to become button-proof by learning to brush things off, walk away, ignore, or dismiss potentially irritating comments, gestures, or behavior. When someone pushes your buttons, don't react as you usually do. Instead, take a moment to think "Here's another opportunity to avoid feeling bothered," and then let it go. Each time you are button-proof is a moment when you're leaving the small stuff to someone else.

Could you be button-proof in the following situations?

1. Your sibling knows that he can annoy you by humming when you're busy or trying to concentrate, so he makes a point of doing it at those times. Your first response is usually

_____.

Your button-proof response is

_____.

2. Your mother knows that you dress the way you want to and don't like her criticizing your choices. Still, she comments on what you wear. Your first response is usually

_____.

Your button-proof response is

_____ .

3. Your best friend knows you don't like to gossip, but still she tries. Your first response is usually

_____ .

Your button-proof response is

_____ .

4. A friend of yours is never ready to go when the rest of the group is. He's going to make you late for the movie *again*, and your response is usually

_____ .

Your button-proof response is

_____ .

What are your buttons? If you know your buttons, you can easily button-proof yourself. Think about the things that annoy, upset, bother, or irritate you. List them here.

_____

_____

_____

_____

_____

_____

How might you button-proof yourself against these things? Think about some button-proof reactions to these things and write them down here.

_____

_____

_____

_____

_____

46

TRUST YOUR INNER SIGNALS

Your inner signal is a foolproof guidance system that lets you know whether you're on track or off track. The signal is your own feelings, and it can tell you if you're doing all right, or if you're headed toward stress, confusion, conflict, and other mental woes. There's a powerful connection between your thoughts and your feelings. Learning to listen to your feelings can help you keep on track most of the time.

Learn to recognize the inner signals that tell you when you're having negative thoughts. Do you listen to your negative feelings? Here is a list of feelings. Check the ones that you remember feeling in the past six months, note when you felt that way and what you did about it.

_____ Self-centered _____

_____ Sad _____

_____ Depressed _____

_____ Annoyed _____

_____ Impatient _____

_____ Anxious _____

_____ Fearful _____

_____ Jealous _____

_____ Angry _____

_____ Grumpy _____

_____ Bored _____

_____ Indifferent _____

_____ Ashamed _____

_____ Regretful _____

47

TAKE TIME OUT TO
WATCH THE SUN SET

It may sound corny, but watching a sunset really can be one of the most powerful and simple things you can do to improve your life. Teenagers are often too busy to appreciate the life that goes on around them. When you learn to take time to observe nature's beauty—whether it's a sunset, a sunrise, a snowfall, or a gentle rain—you're learning to slow down and appreciate life in the moment. Over time, you'll find that such simple diversions can work a sort of magic to make you less stressed, more calm, and more relaxed. You'll appreciate them so much that you'll be far less inclined to search for artificial or harmful ways to create this magic. Best of all, those around you can be influenced by your attitude.

Get into sunsets! Start by doing the following.

1. Pick a good place to watch the sun set—a park, the shore, from your backyard or porch. Check your local newspaper for the exact time of sunset, and then plan to be at your special sunset-watching place at least twenty minutes beforehand.
2. Sunsets can inspire you. Bring a notebook, a tape recorder, a camera, paints and watercolor paper, or some other way to record the sunset or your thoughts and feelings about it. Use this space to jot down feelings, if you wish.

_____

_____

_____

3. You can also just sit back, relax, and soak up all the brilliance of the sunset. If you wish, simply sit quietly and watch, listen, and feel the experience.
4. Sunsets seem to be made for sharing. Bring a friend, a family member, or a significant other, and give yourself a period of stillness in your day.
5. Sunsets can help you realize that life is an incredible gift to be treasured. Once the sun has set, when your mind is clear and peaceful, jot down some things in life for which you're grateful. You can write them in the following space.

_____

_____

_____

6. Make your sunset viewing a personal ritual. Can you do it once a week? Twice?

48

READ A MINIMUM OF
EIGHT PAGES A DAY

❋ To read eight pages a day (above and beyond required school reading) takes only a few minutes, but over time, it really adds up. Think about it: Over a single year, reading eight pages a day comes to almost three thousand pages! In ten years, that's thirty thousand pages! Why read at least eight pages a day? Because reading is a tremendous way to learn, relax, and even escape. The more you read, the more you learn to love it. Becoming smarter doesn't happen overnight, but you can start—eight pages at a time each day.

Expand your mind with reading. While you're at it, try reading something a little different from what you're used to reading. What better way to learn something new? Here are some suggestions. Check off any that you like.

_____ Read a magazine about a sport that you've never tried.

_____ Read a health and fitness magazine.

_____ Read a money and finance magazine.

_____ Read a book about a religion that's different from yours.

_____ Read a book about a faraway country.

_____ Read a biography about a famous historical figure.

_____ Read an art magazine.

_____ Read a magazine about national politics.

_____ Read a book about how to improve yourself in some way.

_____ Read a western novel.

_____ Read a science fiction novel.

_____ Read about World War I.

_____ Read a great work of literature.

_____ Read about space flight.

_____ Read about fashion design.

Can you think of other topics that might interest you? Add them to your list.

_____

_____

_____

_____

_____

49

MAKE SPACE IN YOUR HEART
FOR THOSE REALLY BAD DAYS

Everyone has bad days—and sometimes they're *really* bad. Making space in your heart for those really bad days helps to keep them in perspective and to make them seem more manageable. How can you do that? By understanding that no one is happy all the time. It's like accepting rainy days. You don't freak out when it rains. You wait for the clouds to clear and the sun to emerge. Acceptance is at the root of not sweating the small stuff. It won't stop you from having those bad days, but it will help you get through them more easily.

What did you do the last time you had a really bad day? Reflect on how you handled it, and how you might handle it better in the future. Fill in the following statements about bad days you've had, what you did, and what you might do.

1. I had a really bad day this week. It went like this:

_____

_____

_____

_____

How I handled it:

_____

_____

_____

_____

How I could have handled it better:

_____

_____

_____

_____

2. I had a really bad day last week or last month. It went like this:

_____

_____

_____

_____

How I handled it:

_____

_____

_____

_____

How I could have handled it better:

_____

_____

_____

_____

50

DON'T SWEAT THE FUTURE

* You can guarantee your best possible future by making today all it can be. Teens sometimes feel urgency and fear because they don't know what's going to happen in the future. Career, college, relationships, living arrangements—these are things that lie in your future that can bring you anxiety or excitement. If you do your best every day, the future will take care of itself, and that right there takes away your worries.

What worries you about the future? Write it down. You can take the power away from it by putting it on paper.

Bring your attention to the present. How can you make today the best possible day? Try this exercise.

1. Make a list of the things you've been putting off until someday. They might include cleaning out your closet or sending a thank-you note to someone who has been good to you.
2. Can you accomplish any of the things on your list now, today? Circle the ones you think you can do today.
3. Look at the items you haven't circled. Beside each one, note a day that you plan to start it. While you won't sweat your future, you can make some plans for it.
4. Try to stick to your list. By accomplishing something each day, you not only make it the best day that you can, but you also keep yourself in the present so that you don't sweat the future.

51

EXPERIENCE
VIBRANT HEALTH

✱ The young adult body is strong. But many teens fill themselves with junk food and fail to get enough exercise. That's like handicapping a runner by making him or her wear ankle weights! Feel fantastic rather than okay by taking care of yourself and learning as much as you can about good health.

Make a commitment to start getting healthy today! See your doctor or physical education teacher if you need help with a plan. Take an inventory of your health habits first to see where you stand. You can take this with you to the doctor.

EXERCISE
1. What do you do for exercise? Check off any that apply.

_____ Walk

_____ Run or jog

_____ Swim

_____ Lift weights

_____ Ride a bicycle

_____ Skate or skateboard

_____ Play sports

_____ Ride horses

_____ Go kayaking or canoeing

2. Below, add to your exercise list any other things you do.

_____

_____

_____

3. There are little things you can do to get more exercise in your life. Check these off as you get into the habit of doing them.

_____ Walk to school instead of taking the bus

_____ Park the car at the far end of the lot

_____ Take stairs instead of the elevator

_____ Walk the dog or the neighbor's dog

_____ Mow lawns for others regularly

_____ Take out the trash nightly

DIET

1. What do you typically eat every day? You may be surprised if you write it all down.

Breakfast: _____

Lunch: _____

Dinner: _____

Snacks: _____

2. Do you eat a lot of junk food and sweets? Look at your food list above. Can you substitute something healthier for any of your junk-food snacks? Try one of the following instead.
   • Fruit
   • Piece of cheese
   • Handful of nuts

- Roasted soybeans
- Tomato slice
- Peanut butter on a cracker
- Celery and carrot sticks
- Cucumber slices
- Veggie juice
- Fruit juice
- Small salad
- Whole grain cereal

Can you think of other healthy snacks? List them here.

_____

_____

_____

_____

3. Do you drink enough water? Water is extremely important to good health. Try to drink eight eight-ounce glasses a day. Try substituting a glass of water for a soft drink. Keep track of how many glasses you're drinking a day for an entire week.

Monday _____

Tuesday _____

Wednesday _____

Thursday _____

Friday _____

Saturday _____

Sunday _____

4. Do you take vitamins? List what you take.

_____

_____

SLEEP

1. How much sleep do you get each night? Look at the past week and note how many hours of sleep you got each night.

Monday _____

Tuesday _____

Wednesday _____

Thursday _____

Friday _____

Saturday _____

Sunday _____

2. Did you get less than you thought? Why don't you get enough sleep? Write down the reasons. See if you can adjust your schedule to allow more rest.

_____

_____

_____

_____

_____

STRESS REDUCTION

1. How do you unwind? Stress is a contributing factor to poor health. If you don't have a stress-reduction plan, consider any of the following stress-busting techniques:

_____ Take up yoga

_____ Learn meditation

_____ Listen to calming music

_____ Watch a sunset

_____ Watch a sunrise

_____ Try to resolve problems daily

_____ Stay optimistic

_____ Limit caffeine intake

_____ Keep your weight healthy

_____ Do something fun

_____ Manage time effectively

_____ Release negative emotions

What other ways can you think of to reduce stress? List them.

_____

_____

_____

_____

_____

Write down any questions you want to ask your doctor about how you can be more healthy.

_____

_____

_____

_____

52

VISIT THE ELDERLY

❋ If you want to learn about life, spend some time with those who have the most life experience: the elderly. Visit your grandparents or other people's grandparents, elderly neighbors, or nursing home residents on a regular basis. Ask plenty of questions, and really *listen* to their answers. It's a great way to enrich your life and brighten theirs.

What can you talk about when you visit the elderly? Here are some questions you might ask once you get to know someone. Most elderly people are happy to share their life experiences with younger generations. Think of some more questions to add to the list.

1. Where did you grow up, and what was it like when you were a child?
2. Where did you go to school?
3. What do you think is the most significant change in the world that you've seen over the years?
4. What's your favorite kind of music?
5. When you were my age, who were the popular celebrities?
6. What kind of clothes did you wear at my age?
7. Who's the most incredible person you have ever met?
8. What are some of the most important things that you've learned in life?

How can you make an elderly person's day brighter? You might bring a favorite baked treat, watch a TV show together, go for a walk, or read poetry. Most often, just taking an interest in what an elderly person has to say will be enough.

53

BE AWARE OF THE LAW
OF DIMINISHING RETURNS

❋ Even if you love chocolate sundaes, eating three of them in a row might make you sick. There are many great things in life, but like too many sundaes, you can have too much of a good thing. At some point, a behavior can even work against you. Becoming aware of this "law of diminishing returns" can help you prevent many of the most stress-creating habits in life. You can learn when to back off and ease up.

Is the law of diminishing returns working against you? Check off any of the following that apply, and reflect on your answers.

_____ I'm good at certain things, but often I take on too many of them.

_____ When I want something from my parents, I usually push them too hard.

_____ I like friends, and I have dozens of them.

_____ I love staying up late, but I'm always tired the next day.

_____ I'm not perfect, but I focus on my imperfections a lot.

_____ I want to date someone, but I may be pursuing too hard.

_____ I love playing piano, but I get frustrated when I can't get each piece right.

_____ I'm trying to be well-rounded, but I do a lot and have no time to relax.

_____ I'm trying to eat healthier, but I may be skipping good foods that I need.

_____ I like extra spending money, but I take on too many after-school jobs.

_____ My friends ask my advice, but I have to be careful not to go overboard.

_____ I want my best friend to do things with me, but I may push too much.

_____ I like coffee, but I drink so much that it keeps me awake at night.

_____ I'm into exercise, but I think I hurt myself by overdoing it.

_____ There's so much to learn on the Internet, but I'm getting eyestrain.

_____ I love helping people, but find that I can't say no to anyone.

_____ I like people, but maybe I trust others too much and let them hurt me.

_____ I like giving gifts to people, but I may spend too much and do it too often.

_____ I'm into sports, but I try to play on every team that I can.

_____ I stand up for myself, but I might come on too strong sometimes.

Are there other things in your life that you may do to excess? Be honest. Write about them. How might you back off?

54

DEVELOP YOUR PRESENCE

✳ Presence is a magical, almost magnetic, quality that makes you someone others want to be with. If you have presence, those around you feel special, attended to, and respected because you can make them feel like the most important people in the world. Developing your presence can improve all of your relationships, from those with parents and siblings to those with teachers, employers, friends, and strangers—even your boyfriend or girlfriend. The stronger your presence, the more you'll bring out the best in others.

You can be someone others want to be with if you begin by being open to others. How open are you to others? Take this quiz and find out. Answer *yes, sometimes,* or *no* to each one.

_____ 1. I believe kids younger than me have little to offer me in conversations.

_____ 2. I believe older people have little to offer me in conversations.

_____ 3. I try to avoid people who are physically different from me.

_____ 4. I try to avoid people who I think aren't attractive.

_____ 5. I try to avoid people who dress differently from me.

_____ 6. I often think I know what someone's going to say before he or she says it.

_____ 7. If someone interrupts me, I get very upset.

_____ 8. My opinion counts more than anyone else's.

_____ 9. If I'm an expert in something, I can't learn anything else about it from anyone else.

_____ 10. I can't learn anything from people of other religious faiths.

_____ 11. People who aren't interested in the same things that I am can't possibly understand me.

_____ 12. At gatherings, I like to be the center of attention.

_____ 13. If I don't understand what someone is saying, I pretend that I do rather than ask questions.

_____ 14. I don't want to waste time listening to explanations of things that are obvious.

_____ 15. If someone says something that I know is wrong, I have to interrupt and correct him or her.

If you answered yes or sometimes more than you answered no, you need to work on your presence. You must seek to understand others better.

55

REMIND YOURSELF
THAT NO ONE
IS OUT TO GET YOU

❋ The teen years are often bumpy, and it can seem as if someone is always out to get you. We act like victims, feeling sorry for ourselves, or walk around with chips on our shoulders, acting suspicious, cynical, or paranoid. This heavyhearted attitude takes an enormous toll on our sense of well-being and our experience of life. It robs us of enthusiasm, inspiration, wisdom, and creativity. Accept the fact that while you're a unique individual, in many ways, you're just like everyone else, and no one is out to get you.

Have you ever felt that someone was out to get you? Think of a time when you thought that each of the following people treated you unfairly, did something that wasn't nice, or said the wrong thing. Do you really think they were out to get you, or might the situation have had little or nothing to do with you? Write about each one.

1. Parent

_____

What it probably meant

_____

2. Sibling

_____

What it probably meant

_____

3. Teacher

_____

What it probably meant

_____

4. Friend

_____

What it probably meant

_____

5. Boyfriend/girlfriend

_____

What it probably meant

_____

6. Boss

_____

What it probably meant

_____

7. Coworker

_____

What it probably meant

_____

8. Store clerk

_____

What it probably meant

_____

9. Coach

_____

What it probably meant

_____

10. Teammate

_____

What it probably meant

_____

56

GO THE EXTRA MILE

❋ If you always wonder what the payoff will be for your efforts, you may end up thinking and feeling "Why bother?" Remember that giving your best effort to whatever you do often brings rewards from unexpected sources. We build our lives one day at a time, much like a carpenter builds a house. But if you put less than your best effort into it, you'll live in a shoddy house. The attitude and choices you make today build the house that you will live in tomorrow. Go the extra mile and give life your best shot—you'll build a life you can be proud of.

Do you go the extra mile, and do you do it with enthusiasm? Take this quiz to find out. Decide which statement in each group best describes you. Write the point value in the space beside the statement.

1. When I'm given a new project at school, I

_____ look forward to the challenge and think of ways I can do it really well. (3)

_____ take on the project but figure out how I can do it with the least amount of effort. (2)

_____ look for reasons why I can't do the project at all. (1)

2. I join the class softball team even though I haven't played the game much before. I

_____ go to every practice, and toss the ball around with friends when I have extra time. (3)

_____ skip a lot of practices and make excuses why I couldn't be there. (1)

_____ go to practice, but I don't do much unless I have to. (2)

3. Mom asks me to go through my closet and find things that I don't use anymore that we can donate to charity. I

_____ look in the closet briefly, then tell her that I can't find anything. (1)

_____ pick carefully through everything, rearrange all the clothes, and clean up the messy floor while I put things in a box for charity. (3)

_____ grab some clothing items and some unused sports equipment and give it to her. (2)

4. I sign up for Spanish classes because I think it would be fun and useful. I

_____ read the textbook, go on the Internet to find sites that teach common phrases, and watch the Spanish-language TV station every now and then. (3)

_____ do my homework regularly and do well. (2)

_____ give it a shot and decide it's too difficult to bother with. (1)

SCORING:

4–6: You don't even go the first mile let alone the extra one. You should learn to take pride in everything you do. Not only is a job well done worth doing, but it's worth giving your all and more to do the best job you can.

7–9: You get the job done, but no more.

10–12: You give it your all—and more! You really know how to go the extra mile.

Now look back at each of the items and ask yourself: What's the payoff? Jot down what you think might happen if you went the extra mile in each case. Use your imagination.

1. _____

2. _____

3. _____

4. _____

57

WATCH YOUR LANGUAGE

❋ The words you use to express yourself and the things you choose to talk about play an important role in the overall quality of your life. If you pay attention to how much you talk, use foul language, or think about things like violence, greed, and sex, you may be surprised. The power of your words and thoughts is tremendous. You can choose to direct it toward things that promote happiness.

You don't have to put your head in the sand and *never* talk about unpleasant things. Just pay closer attention to what you say and think. Try this experiment, and check off each of these six items after you accomplish them. Write down any thoughts you have or things you've learned after the experiment.

_____ Go an entire day without swearing.

_____ Try not to criticize anyone or anything for two days in a row.

_____ Don't play any violent video games for an entire weekend.

_____ Spend an entire evening with a friend, or friends, and don't talk about sex.

_____ Watch nonviolent programs on TV for forty-eight hours.

_____ For three days, notice every time you say to yourself "I want . . ."

58

BE CREATIVE
IN YOUR REBELLION

✳ There's nothing really wrong with rebellion; the problem is often the *form* that rebellion takes. We rebel when we're unhappy, dissatisfied, or discontented. The media tells us that we can't be happy unless we use their products or watch their shows, and that our lives will be better if we do. But you don't have to buy the right stuff or look different to be happy. Making your own decision to be happy just the way you are is the ultimate form of rebellion.

Be rebellious by being happy with what you have instead of what you want. Do you focus too much on what you *don't* have? Take this true/false quiz and find out where you need some work.

1. I'm generally happy with what I have.   T   F

2. When I buy something, I keep in mind how much it will impress everyone.   T   F

3. I have to get the newest and latest things, because they're always better.   T   F

4. Sometimes "new and improved" or "better" things can disappoint.   T   F

5. People are never satisfied with what they have.   T   F

6. I work hard to achieve things, but once I get them, I'm usually disappointed.   T   F

7. I'd be happier if I had nicer, more expensive things.   T   F

8. I sometimes get jealous of what my friends do or have.   T   F

9. I'd go into debt if I had to in order to get something I really wanted.   T   F

10. I see myself years from now as a very happy person.   T   F

1. Make a list of things that bring you happiness.
2. What was your life like before you had these things? Is there anything on the list that you were once content to live without? Circle it. Do these items have anything in common?
3. Now list things that you wanted that ended up disappointing you rather than making you happy. Do these things have something in common?
4. Are you jealous of something that a friend has? Jot it down. Does it make your friend a happier or better person than you? Is there something that you have that this person doesn't have? Would you ever trade places with this person?

59

LET PEOPLE TALK

Almost all people love to talk more than they love to listen. We have a need to be heard, and if we aren't, we feel that something's missing. If others hear us, we feel nourished and satisfied. Understandably, you probably enjoy people who take time to listen and don't interrupt you. Others will like you, too, if you practice the art of listening. That's the key to great relationships—allowing others times to talk while you listen well.

The best listeners wait until others are finished speaking before responding. They pause, take a breath, and then speak. How do you behave in conversation with others? Find out with this quiz. Score 0 for *never*, 5 for *sometimes*, and 10 for *most of the time*.

_____ 1. Do you interrupt others when they're speaking?

_____ 2. Do you finish sentences for others who are speaking?

_____ 3. Do you say "I know" a lot when others are speaking?

_____ 4. Can you barely contain yourself from wanting to jump in and say your piece?

_____ 5. Do pauses in conversation make you feel uncomfortable?

_____ 6. Do you say "You've said that before" to someone who's trying to explain something?

_____ 7. Do you ever feel that you annoy or irritate people when you're talking with them?

_____ 8. Do you criticize others' viewpoints before they've finished speaking?

SCORING:

Less than 20: You're an unhurried communicator, and people likely enjoy talking with you.

Between 20 and 60: You don't have much patience and probably don't pay much attention to what's being said. People may avoid talking with you.

Over 60: You're no fun to talk with! Does anyone talk with you?

Which of the above responses relates to something you'd like to change about how you listen and communicate? Circle each one, and write below how you might improve your skills.

_____

_____

_____

60

REFLECT ON THE MAP

You live on a big, beautiful planet filled with diverse, interesting people. When you're aware of—and care about—these people and what they're going through, you feel connected to others, and your own problems are put into perspective. Expanding your vision to encompass the rest of humanity can make your small stuff seem a lot less significant. You can be grateful that you are able to reflect, be aware of what's happening in the world, and feel compassion for others.

Look at a world map and reflect on how people in other countries live. With the help of news reports, the Internet, or the library, see if you can find answers to these questions, and learn as much as you can.

1. Where is a war currently being fought?
2. In what countries are poverty and hunger big problems?
3. Pick a faraway country and ask yourself, "What is life like for the average citizen there?" Find out by doing research.
4. Find a country you would like to visit. Make a list of reasons why you chose this particular country.
5. You've raised your awareness. Can you do anything to help those less fortunate around the world? Find a charity or cause to which you might donate time, money, or goods. You can make a difference.

61

DISH OUT PRAISE

✳ Everyone loves to receive compliments and praise, as long as they're real and sincere. People are interested in what teenagers think. The opinions of youth, especially when they are positive, carry a certain weight. Dishing out praise is a great idea, but few teens do it—they're either too shy or too uncomfortable, or they feel that others don't need to be praised. But it's well worth overcoming this reticence to make an effort to praise and compliment others. There's simply no downside to it, and it will improve your quality of life.

When it's real and deserved, explore the magic of praise. Try the following.

1. Who do you know deserves compliments or praise? List them (friends, teachers, parents, neighbors—whoever you admire). Next to their names, write down why they should be praised or complimented. Perhaps the person is smart, helpful, always there for you, or simply has a great personality.
2. Now, write down a compliment you can say to that person based on what you admire. For example:

   WHO: Mr. Smith, science teacher

   WHY: He always has time for my questions.

   COMPLIMENT: "Mr. Smith, you're always there to help me with my questions. I want you to know that I appreciate that, and I really learn a lot from you."
3. You can praise someone about little things, too. Here's a list of things that you could compliment someone for. Do you know anyone you can praise about these things? Jot down their names beside the items. List other things you can praise.

Personality _____

Smile _____

Sense of humor _____

Laugh _____

Attitude _____

Honesty _____

Hair _____

Clothing _____

Car _____

Love of life _____

Love of work _____

Cooking ability _____

Artistic sense _____

Skills and abilities _____

Tact _____

62

DON'T BURN BRIDGES

✳ Bridges represent connections. If you burn a bridge, you can't get to the other side. Relationships between people are the same way—human bridges can be destroyed and damage relationships beyond repair. To avoid this stress, you may wish to make it your personal goal to never burn a bridge. Keep things in perspective, and don't do anything that will permanently ruin a relationship. If you do burn a bridge and later regret it, it's possible to restore it by reaching out to the other person. Life is about relationships. They are constantly changing, and we can learn from all of them.

1. Have you burned any bridges with friends, family, teachers, employers—anyone? List them.
2. Can you possibly repair any of them? Think about how you might reach out to the other person. Jot down your ideas.
3. Writing a heartfelt letter might be a good place to start restoring a burned bridge. Take a shot at writing such a letter. You don't have to send it. But if you like what you've written and really want to fix that bridge, then send it!
4. Are there any potential burning bridges looming in your future? Write about how you might avoid a big blaze.

63

UNDERSTAND THE
LAW OF FOCUS

✳ Having focus allows thoughts and actions to expand. Teens often benefit from staying focused on a feeling, goal, or simple task at hand. But if you focus on negative ideas, you will cause yourself unwanted stress and unhappiness. Constantly focusing on flaws or mistakes can get you really uptight! Knowing this can help you nip negativity in the bud. If you know that your focus contributes to how you feel, you can be less angry, sad, or annoyed. Focus less on minor annoyances, and the world can be much less upsetting.

Do you focus on the small stuff and make it bigger? Here are some common annoyances on which people tend to focus. Put a checkmark beside the ones you have had. How much do you focus on them? Circle 0 for *not at all*, 1 for *a little*, 2 for *pretty much*, and 3 for *a lot*. Add to the list any other things on which you focus, and rate how much you dwell on them. If you have mostly twos and threes, you need to better understand the law of focus.

_____	1. I hate my clothes.	0	1	2	3
_____	2. I don't like my hair.	0	1	2	3
_____	3. My teacher bugs me.	0	1	2	3
_____	4. My brother/sister gets on my nerves.	0	1	2	3
_____	5. I'm not good at sports.	0	1	2	3
_____	6. I'm not good at math.	0	1	2	3
_____	7. This class I'm taking is a waste of time!	0	1	2	3
_____	8. There's nothing to do in this town.	0	1	2	3
_____	9. I never get what I want.	0	1	2	3
_____	10. I'm bored.	0	1	2	3

_____ 11. My boyfriend/girlfriend doesn't
really love me. 0 1 2 3
_____ 12. My friends don't really like me. 0 1 2 3
_____ 13. I'll mess up at my music recital. 0 1 2 3
_____ 14. If the teacher asks me something
that I don't know, I'll look stupid. 0 1 2 3
_____ 15. Nothing I try works out. 0 1 2 3
_____ 16. Everyone else on the team is out
to get me. 0 1 2 3
_____ 17. I can't wait until I graduate and
leave home. 0 1 2 3
_____ 18. I always wear the wrong thing to
parties. 0 1 2 3
_____ 19. The neighbor is driving me crazy! 0 1 2 3
_____ 20. I hate driving Dad's out-of-date car. 0 1 2 3

64

USE REMINDER CARDS

✳ We sometimes need help reminding ourselves to implement ideas that will make our lives peaceful, productive, and happy. Reminder cards are a great way to do this. Just write down on paper or index cards any thoughts, ideas, or insights that are meaningful to you. Keep them in places where you'll see them, like your backpack, car visor, purse or wallet, inside a book, or next to your bed. They really do help to remind you of positive, life-affirming statements and important ideas, and they reinforce things you deem important.

What would you like to emphasize on your reminder cards? Success, happiness, overcoming adversity, kindness, compassion, grades, friendship—you name it. Jot down some categories.

_____

_____

_____

Come up with positive statements and reminders for each of your categories. Need some help? Use some of the chapter titles of this journal. Here are some other suggestions that you can use.

Life isn't an emergency.

I can choose happiness.

I will look for good and beauty in everything around me.

I'm glad to be a teenager.

Have you shown someone your kindness today?

I can be a role model.

I know that no one is out to get me.

I'm grateful every day for what I have.

Have you let someone know that you're happy for them?

I don't have to be perfect—I can be me.

Am I keeping my sense of humor, especially in bad times?

Remember the best 90 percent today.

65

BE GLAD TO BE A TEEN

✳ Being a teenager is cool! Enjoy it while you can, in spite of the fact that everyone wants you to grow up really fast. Don't buy into that line of thinking—you'll be an adult soon enough. Enjoy where you are right at this moment. Your teenage years are about self-discovery and learning to make your way in the world. They won't be easy, but the difficult times will be matched by a unique freedom and sense of joy.

Are you enjoying all that you should of your teenage years? Score 10 for the statements that you mostly agree with, 5 for those you somewhat agree with, and 0 for those you disagree with.

I'd be happier if

_____ 1. I was out of school.

_____ 2. I lived on my own.

_____ 3. I had my own car.

_____ 4. I could do whatever I wanted with my room.

_____ 5. I didn't have to study anymore.

_____ 6. I didn't have to deal with authority figures.

_____ 7. I lived in a different house.

_____ 8. I lived in a different neighborhood.

_____ 9. I had all new clothes.

_____ 10. I could do what I wanted to do when I wanted to do it.

_____ 11. I was doing something else right now.

_____ 12. my family was easier to get along with.

_____ 13. I was a more important person at school.

_____ 14. I was/was not in a relationship.

_____ 15. I took different classes.

_____ 16. I didn't have so many chores to do.

_____ 17. I was younger again.

_____ 18. I didn't have a curfew.

SCORING

Below 45: You're happy in the present and okay with being a teen.

45–90: You have worries that interfere with being who you are right now.

91–135: You dwell too much on what you're not.

Above 135: You need to find ways to be happier that you're a teen and enjoy your life as a teen.

66

EXPERIENCE DEEP LISTENING

✳ Busy listening, or surface listening, occurs when you have a lot of other things going on in your head while you're listening to someone else. You might be preoccupied with other thoughts, anxiously waiting for your turn to speak, or comparing what you're hearing to what you already know. You're distracted and incapable of giving your full attention. Poor listening is at the heart of many relationship problems. Everyone, especially teens, wants to be "heard." Only then do we feel understood and accepted. Enhance your ability to concentrate, relax, and enjoy listening by clearing your mind. Remember that you have much to learn by listening to others and much to give by doing so.

Learn to become a better listener. The true/false exercise below can help you find your problem areas so that you can work on improving your listening skills.

1. I rarely remember people's names when I first meet them.   T   F

2. I'm always doing something else while talking to someone on the phone.   T   F

3. I let people finish their sentences completely before I speak.   T   F

4. People seek me out to tell me their problems and troubles.   T   F

5. I'm always interested in hearing what someone else has to say.   T   F

6. I usually know what people are going to say
   before they actually say it.   T   F

7. I get impatient when someone speaks slowly to me. T   F

8. My mind wanders when some people talk to me.   T   F

9. I don't make eye contact with people who are
   talking to me.   T   F

10. I cut people off in conversation.   T   F

Who is the best listener you know? Write down why you think this person is a good listener.

_____

_____

_____

_____

As a listener, do you share any qualities with this person? Circle them. The ones that you don't circle are areas you might consider working to improve.

67

BE WARY OF FRIENDS WHO ENCOURAGE YOU TO DWELL

Good friends who listen well are one of life's greater gifts and joys. Good listeners care about you, share your joy and pain, and want you to be happy. Others may seem to be good listeners while actually thriving on your troubles. People like this often cause us to dwell on our problems. If you leave a conversation with a friend feeling more anxious than you were before you started talking, then you may be involved with such a person. This can drain you of energy and cause you great unhappiness.

How can you tell a good listener from someone who encourages you to dwell? Look closely at what they say, and they give themselves away. Read the following quotes and decide if each is being said by a good listener or a dweller. In the space before the sentence, put a G for good listener or a D for dweller.

_____ 1. If I were you, I'd never put up with that!

_____ 2. Don't worry, you'll find a way to get through this—you always do!

_____ 3. I think you're right, and I'll stand behind you, whatever you choose to do.

_____ 4. Doesn't that just really irritate you?

_____ 5. If I were you, I'd be completely nuts by now! I don't know how you stand it!

_____ 6. Take some deep breaths, relax, and we'll figure this out together.

_____ 7. Well, if that's how she feels, you should show her a thing or two.

_____ 8. Listen, let's go cheer up with a movie; I know you'll see things differently later.

_____ 9. That happened to me once, and here's what I did. It worked, and it will work for you, too.

_____ 10. You should make him feel the same pain you're feeling. That'll teach him!

(Statements 2, 3, 6, 8, and 9 are G; the rest are D.)

68

CREATE YOUR OWN
SPECIAL PLACE

✳ Having your own special place to go just to be alone and quiet can be one of the greatest joys in life. Time spent there can be powerful in releasing stress, as well as giving you a place to reflect and meditate, draw or write poetry, or just clear your mind and be still in the moment. Your special place doesn't have to be fancy, but it does have to be your own, where you can go to be alone and find peace and inner happiness.

Where can you create your own special place? Here are some suggestions. Check them out, and see if one of them can work for you. Add your own ideas to the list.

Your room

A closet

The attic

A room in the basement

A tree house

A shed

A place in the garden

An area of the yard

Under the stairs

A barn

A certain bench in a park

A place by a pond or lake

Under a huge tree

A certain grove of trees

A courtyard

A meadow

Once you've found your special place, how will you use it? List the ways—anything from creating art, praying, or meditating to sitting quietly, doing nothing.

69

REMEMBER TO BE
GRATEFUL

❋ Remembering to be grateful has the power to change your life. Being grateful means thinking more about what you have and what's right with your life than about what's wrong, what's missing, or what could be better. It also means expressing your gratitude to others for what they mean to you and do for you. Keeping a gratitude journal where you record what is good about your day, your life, and yourself can help with this. You can begin here.

Take this quiz. Select the statement that best reflects you and write the point value in the space.

1. Everyone compliments me on my smooth, clear skin. I

_____ thank them graciously and take good care of my skin. (2)

_____ point out that I weigh too much and my hair is frizzy. (1)

2. A teacher congratulates me on getting ninety-five on a test. I

_____ say "Thanks"; I'm proud of how well I did. (2)

_____ say, "Thanks. I don't know why I didn't get them all right." (1)

3. I had a perfect day until I slipped and fell into a mud puddle on the way home from school. At the dinner table, I

_____ go on and on about how I ruined my clothes and felt embarrassed by falling. (1)

_____ tell everyone about my good day at school. (2)

4. A neighbor leaves a card at my house to thank me for helping him last week. In the card is a ten-dollar bill. I

_____ didn't expect to get paid, and I'm thrilled. I call right away and thank him. (2)

_____ didn't expect to get paid, but I wonder why he's being so cheap. (1)

5. My friend's parents are splitting up. She's upset and cries. I

_____ tell her that at least she'll have one less parent around to tell her what to do. (1)

_____ try to make her feel better. I'm lucky I have two great parents. (2)

SCORING

5–7: Oops! You need to focus more on what's right with your life and be grateful for what you've got.

8–10: You have an attitude of gratitude.

Try this experiment: When you wake up each day this week, think of three things that you have to be grateful for. They can be anything, from being healthy to having understanding parents to having a car of your own. Write them down. This can help you to remember daily how much you have to be grateful for. Use the space below for your answers.

Monday: I'm grateful for

1. _____.

2. _____.

3. _____.

Tuesday: I'm grateful for

1. _____.

2. _____.

3. _____.

Wednesday: I'm grateful for

1. _____.

2. _____.

3. _____.

Thursday: I'm grateful for

1. _____.

2. _____.

3. _____.

Friday: I'm grateful for

1. _____.

2. _____.

3. _____.

Saturday: I'm grateful for

1. _____.

2. _____.

3. _____.

Sunday: I'm grateful for

1. _____.

2. _____.

3. _____.

70

READ THE FINE PRINT

❋ Sometimes we make assumptions about the way things should be without even realizing we're doing it. We think our ideas and beliefs are obvious and correct, and that everyone else sees things the same way we do. These invisible assumptions are like the fine print in a document—difficult to read but a catalyst for misunderstanding if you don't. Reading the fine print in others' behavior is difficult. Sometimes we don't even understand our own fine print. Frustration and pain can result if we are unaware of the true motivations and value of our behavior. Learning to identify and delete some of your own fine print can eliminate a great deal of stress and disappointment.

What does your fine print say? Often, it spells out your expectations. If things don't go as you expect, you're disappointed. Or you make leading assumptions about yourself that aren't necessarily valid. Be open to what eliminates expectations and deletes the fine print, making life a lot happier and stress-free.

Take this quiz to see if you can understand your own fine print. Check off the statements you believe are true about how you think and feel, and give yourself a point for each one.

_____ If I lose at any game I play, it means I'm a loser in general.

_____ I have to get those expensive shoes, or no one will like me.

_____ If you don't do this for me, I'll break up with you.

_____ How could my parents have embarrassed me like that?

_____ If you don't agree with me, then don't bother telling me what you think.

_____ I'm not going to the party unless I find out who's going to be there.

_____ The dentist made me wait for an hour, and I'm really steamed!

_____ No one appreciates how hard I have to work to get a good grade.

_____ I gave my boyfriend/girlfriend a wonderful gift, and he/she barely noticed it!

_____ I won't join the team because I'm just not a good player.

_____ I'm going to dye my hair as soon as I'm allowed.

_____ My idea of what we should do tonight is better than your idea.

_____ Those kids did that just to spite me.

_____ This day is great, and nothing's going to ruin it.

_____ I don't believe you said that. You must be joking.

_____ This team would win more games if I were the captain and made the decisions.

_____ If they'd have given me a break, I would have shown them that I could be a great cheerleader.

SCORING:

Less than 5: You're pretty open to "what is" and don't have much fine print at all.

5–9: You take the world as it comes the majority of the time.

10–14: You've got some fine print, for sure.

More than 14: You've got a lot of fine print to delete, and you'd be happier without it.

71

LOOK FOR THE INNOCENCE

✳ People make mistakes—it's only human. Most people are doing the best they can to make it through their days, just like you. Sometimes they do things that annoy or irritate you—cut you off on the road, say the wrong thing, spill something, make too much noise, or forget to say thank you. They don't do it intentionally and don't mean you harm. They have simply messed up, as you do sometimes. If you recognize that people can't be at their best all the time, you'll be able to look the other way when something slightly negative crosses your path. You'll keep things in their proper perspective so they don't adversely affect your day.

Can you see the innocence in others? Take this true/false quiz to find out where you can make improvements.

1. If someone yells at me, I take it personally.   T   F

2. I sometimes yell at people even when I know it's not their fault.   T   F

3. If someone's in a bad mood, I get upset and think it's about me.   T   F

4. If someone cuts in front of me on the road, I think he or she is a pushy driver.   T   F

5. There's no excuse for behaving irrationally around others.   T   F

6. Arrogant people are just arrogant.   T   F

7. My first impressions of people are always right.   T   F

8. If someone hurts my feelings, I go away and sulk.   T   F

9. If someone uses something of mine without
   asking me, I'm offended.   T   F

If you answered true to any of these statements, that is an area where you need to look more closely to see the innocence in others.

72

DON'T EXAGGERATE
YOUR TROUBLES

❋ Creating mountains of trouble out of what are really small heaps of frustration will make your life harder than it needs to be. Exaggerating your troubles can become a self-fulfilling prophecy that causes you to focus in on your problems even more. Eventually, you begin to believe in your own oversized dramas. Learn to honestly admit when you're exaggerating your troubles. Then you can see your situation as it really is and know that it's not quite as bad as you think.

Do you exaggerate your troubles? For each situation, fill in (a) how you might react if you exaggerate your problem, and (b) how you might react if you realize that you're exaggerating the situation and it's really not as bad as you first thought.

1. You've called several friends to go do something and no one's home. You feel lonely.

   a. _____

   b. _____

2. You're driving your dad's car, and you scrape the bumper against a tree.

   a. _____

   b. _____

3. You thought you aced the English test, but it turns out that you misread one of the essay questions, and your score is far below what you expected.

a. _____

b. _____

4. Your date to the big dance has to cancel at the last minute due to the flu.

   a. _____

   b. _____

5. You worked on your science project for weeks and finally finished. At the last minute, something goes wrong, and it falls apart.

   a. _____

   b. _____

6. Your boyfriend/girlfriend dumps you.

   a. _____

   b. _____

7. You scrimped and saved to buy something that you've wanted for a long time, and then one of your siblings borrows it and breaks it.

   a. _____

   b. _____

73

DEVELOP A THEME
FOR THE DAY

✳ The simple act of declaring a goal or theme for the day can plant a mental seed that has the suggestive power to make it happen. You can be quite surprised by the results. Having a theme will automatically focus your thoughts. Try gratitude, for example. You'll notice more things about your life to be grateful for than at any other time. Spend a few moments each morning deciding on a theme for the day. Your days will look better and better.

Here are some suggestions for daily themes.

Patience

Kindness

Compassion

Thoughtfulness

Listening

Humor

Making eye contact

Forgiveness

Friendliness

Understanding

Optimism

Concentration

Lightheartedness

Perspective

Relaxation

   Add your own ideas for daily themes.

_____

_____

_____

   Now, plan a week of daily themes using the suggested list and your own ideas. See if you can jot down your thoughts and feelings at the end of each day. Was it a good day? Did you enjoy the theme? Make your schedule and take notes here.

Monday's theme: _____

_____

Tuesday's theme: _____

_____

Wednesday's theme: _____

_____

Thursday's theme: _____

_____

Friday's theme: _____

_____

Saturday's theme: _____

_____

Sunday's theme: _____

_____

74

APPLY THE ONE-TO-TEN SCALE

Many of the things we view as big deals aren't really as important as we make them out to be. You can measure things that bother you on a scale from 1 to 10. When you're feeling stressed out, rating things as 1 (very unimportant) through 10 (very important) can help you find perspective.

When you're upset about something, you'll naturally give it a higher rating. If you think about it again later, however, it is very possible that you will give the issue a lower rating. This new rating is probably more accurate, and you'll find that many problems aren't worth losing sleep over. You'll learn that blowing things out of proportion is a natural human tendency that we can avoid. Here's a procedure to follow whenever something bothers you. Turn to this page and, on another sheet of paper, write the answers to each step.

1. What's bothering me? (For example, my best friend promised to do something and didn't do it.)
2. How important is this to me? (The first time you think about this, you might write "6.")
3. Now walk away for a while. Come back in a few hours.
4. Welcome back! Now, think again: How important is this problem? Cut the number you wrote last time in half. (In the example, it would now be a "3.")
5. Is this the *real* level of importance? Probably! Now you don't feel so bad, do you? Write how you feel now.

If you get into the habit of doing this on paper whenever something bothers you, you'll eventually be able to do it in your head. Pretty soon you'll be sweating the small stuff a whole lot less.

75

REMAIN OPTIMISTIC

✳ People who tend to sweat the small stuff the most are generally pessimistic. They might call themselves realists, but the only reality they're focusing on is what's wrong with their lives or the world. You can choose to be optimistic and focus on what's right with the world. Don't worry, you don't have to be unrealistic—you can acknowledge the problems and pain in the world. Simply don't let yourself get bogged down by negativity—you can do more to solve your problems, make your life less stressful, and be happier.

Find out if you're an optimist or if you tend to focus on the injustices in your life by doing this true/false exercise. Reflect on your answers.

1. It's healthy to believe that the best is yet to come. T   F

2. Everyone has the power to change their attitude about the world.   T   F

3. Life can be difficult sometimes, and not so difficult at other times.   T   F

4. Money, fame, and privilege can't buy happiness.   T   F

5. I think I get a lot of good breaks in life.   T   F

6. When the chips are down, I know they won't be down for long.   T   F

7. I can usually make the best of most any circumstance.   T   F

8. Sometimes you just have to laugh at yourself.   T   F

9. Sometimes you have to cry—then you feel better.   T   F

1. Write down any situations where others seemed to freak out but you kept your cool and were optimistic about the outcome.

_____

_____

_____

2. Are you struggling with some problems right now? Can you be optimistic about how they'll be resolved? Write about them and your feelings toward them.

_____

_____

_____

76

EMPATHIZE

Learning to empathize is a great way to become a more gracious, thoughtful, and happier person. When you empathize with people, you put yourself in their shoes to better understand things from their perspective. The opposite of empathy is indifference, which is a more selfish way of thinking and acting. Empathy is easy to develop—all it takes is a willingness to see things from another's point of view. Teenagers are often accused of being self-involved, but no one who feels empathy for others is guilty of this.

Can you empathize with others? What actions might that lead to? Look at these situations.

1. A new kid at school is awkward and lonely. He has no friends and no one to talk to. How would you feel if you were him?

_____

_____

_____

Knowing this, what might you do to help him feel better?

_____

_____

_____

2. Your friend's boyfriend breaks up with her right before the big dance. He's asked another girl to go with him. Your friend is very hurt and angry and says she'd rather stay home. How would you feel if you were her?

_____

_____

_____

She doesn't want to see her ex-boyfriend at the dance with another girl. What might you do to help her feel better?

_____

_____

3. Your friend's pet has passed away and she's extremely upset. She cries and cries. Some kids tell her she's a crybaby and say "Grow up." How would you feel if you were her?

_____

_____

_____

What might you do to help her feel better?

_____

_____

_____

Think of some other situations where you might help someone by understanding what he or she is feeling. Jot your ideas down.

_____

_____

_____

_____

77

LOOK WHO'S DOING YOGA

✳ It may not sound like something for teenagers, but practicing yoga can help you create a more peaceful body, mind, and spirit. It's simple, relaxing, easy to learn, and fun. It's a series of poses and stretches that energize your body, leaving you feeling calm, balanced, and focused. Many entertainers, athletes, and important businesspeople practice yoga to give them a sense of calm and control over their busy lives. You can learn yoga from books or videos, or by taking classes. Teens have to deal with many issues and responsibilities—schoolwork, family life, and peer pressure, to name a few. Yoga may help you balance these things. Still not convinced? You may have some misconceptions about yoga. Take this true/false quiz and find out.

1. I think yoga is too hard for me to learn.   T   F

2. I don't have enough time to do yoga—
   it takes too long.   T   F

3. I'm not athletic, so I can't do yoga.   T   F

4. I can't afford to join the gym or pay a trainer,
   so I can't learn yoga.   T   F

5. I can't buy the equipment needed for yoga.   T   F

6. There's no room at our house for me to do yoga.   T   F

7. The other kids will think I'm weird if I do yoga.   T   F

The correct answer for every question is false. Each statement is a popular misconception about yoga.

Below is a list of the benefits of yoga. Check off those you would like to do. You may quickly convince yourself to give yoga a try.

_____ Strengthen my muscles.

_____ Make my body more flexible.

_____ Clear and quiet my mind.

_____ Make me feel happy and peaceful.

_____ Reduce my stress.

_____ Give me more energy.

_____ Allow me to be quietly with myself each day.

_____ Improve my mental focus and concentration.

78

BE CAREFUL THAT YOU'RE NOT PRACTICING BEING UNHAPPY

You can actually practice being unhappy by giving in to negative thoughts and allowing them to make you behave badly. Your state of mind will affect the way you show yourself to the world. When negative thinking becomes a habit, you become that which you practice most. Teens can easily fall into this trap. The teenage years are often a time of insecurity and doubt, and those feelings can take over. Instead, nip your negative thoughts, or "thought attacks," in the bud, and choose to bring forth better behavior by practicing to be happy.

Are you practicing to be unhappy or happy? Take this quiz and find out. Read each sentence, and then check the emotion that you would most likely feel in that situation.

1. You're given a new project in computer class, and it's a tough one.
angry ___ sad ___ stressed ___ happy ___ accepting ___ understanding ___

2. A kid at school insults you.
angry ___ sad ___ stressed ___ happy ___ accepting ___ understanding ___

3. Your parents want you to get a haircut.
angry ___ sad ___ stressed ___ happy ___ accepting ___ understanding ___

4. You and your best friend have a big disagreement.
angry ___ sad ___ stressed ___ happy ___ accepting ___ understanding ___

5. One of your classmates takes credit for an idea that you had first.
angry ___ sad ___ stressed ___ happy ___ accepting ___ understanding ___

Add up your checkmarks. If you checked mostly *happy*, *accepting*, and *understanding*, then you're a practitioner of the art of being happy, content, and peaceful.

If you checked mostly *angry*, *sad*, or *stressed*, those are negative responses, and you seem to be practicing to be unhappy. You should try to practice more positive responses to what's happening in your life and the people around you.

79

CUT YOUR LOSSES

✳ Everyone makes mistakes, says the wrong thing, or goofs up once in awhile. It's part of being human. How you react to making mistakes can cause more stress than the mistakes themselves. If you can admit to mistakes, make apologies when necessary, and be graceful about it, you'll probably be okay. But if you make excuses, blame others, get defensive, or run away from the problem, you'll have blown it up even further. Hold your head up and cut your losses. Learn from your mistakes, and others will respect you for it.

Look at the following mistakes, and see what lessons you might learn from each.

MISTAKE:
    I made a hurtful, insensitive remark about a person—and he heard me.
LESSON:

_____

_____

MISTAKE:
    I cheated on a quiz—and got caught.
LESSON:

_____

_____

MISTAKE:

I lost my temper at team practice—and the coach benched me for two games.

LESSON:

_____

_____

MISTAKE:

My friend loaned me something, and I didn't take care of it. I have to buy a new one.

LESSON:

_____

_____

MISTAKE:

I promised to help my brother/sister with a school project, but I went out instead.

LESSON:

_____

_____

MISTAKE:

My friend was in the hospital for a week, but I never went to visit.

LESSON:

_____

_____

MISTAKE:

My parents trusted me to be home alone, but I partied, and things got out of hand.

LESSON:

_____

_____

MISTAKE:

I usually do my own thing, but I followed the wrong crowd and got into trouble.

LESSON:

_____

_____

80

EXAMINE YOUR HEADLINES

❋ Just as newspapers have headline stories to grab your attention, so do our personal lives. Our personal headlines are stories and personality traits that we focus on, emphasize, and present to others. Often, they are how we define ourselves, but sometimes we don't even know what our most prominent headlines are!

Maybe you're a busy person, or a studious one—or maybe you're a jock, a car nut, or a shopping fiend. Headlines aren't always bad, often they're wonderful. Examine your own headlines, not to be critical of yourself but to know what they are. Maybe you'll want to make changes, and maybe not. You may surprise yourself.

Extra! Extra! Read all about it! What are *your* personal headlines? Here are some possibilities. Do any of them ring true for you?

Nice guy/girl

Teacher's pet

Jock

Rocker

Rocket scientist

Gloomy

Usually ticked off

Everyone's friend

Helpful

Troublemaker

Busy

Bored

Smart-aleck

Class clown

Mr. or Miss Personality

Bohemian

Creative

Logical

Fashion hound

Trendsetter

Crowd leader

Crowd follower

Health conscious

Artistic

What's your worst headline? What's your best? Write them down. How would you change them if you wanted to?

81

NOTICE YOUR PARENTS
DOING THINGS RIGHT

Many teens wish that their parents would pay less attention to what they do wrong and more attention to what they do right. This works both ways. You may complain about what your parents do wrong and not give them any credit for what they're doing right. Both teens and parents are better motivated by positive reinforcement than by negative words—everyone responds better to praise than to criticism. If you notice more of what your parents are doing right than wrong, they just may return the favor.

What are your parents doing right? If you think about it, probably plenty! Keep track of their actions for one week and you'll begin to appreciate what your parents do right, even if you think they do some things wrong, too.

MONDAY

Today, my parents did these things *right*:

_____

_____

TUESDAY

Today, my parents did these things *right*:

_____

_____

WEDNESDAY

Today, my parents did these things *right*:

_____

_____

THURSDAY

Today, my parents did these things *right*:

_____

_____

FRIDAY

Today, my parents did these things *right*:

_____

_____

SATURDAY

Today, my parents did these things *right*:

_____

_____

SUNDAY

Today, my parents did these things *right*:

_____

_____

82

BECOME A LITTLE
LESS STUBBORN

❊ Stubbornness is easy for others to see but difficult to detect in ourselves. Being stubborn means that you probably sweat the small stuff a lot. Because of your closed mind and unwillingness to listen to others, things will irritate you more easily. If you can learn to soften your position a bit and open your mind, you'll feel free, and others will notice the change in you right away. People enjoy being around someone who isn't stubborn. Learning to say "You're right" to others shows that you're willing to listen and learn.

Are you stubborn about certain things? Write down three positions that you are particularly stubborn about (for example, "Parents don't care about what teenagers want"). List why you have been reluctant to give each one up ("I'd be admitting that when they won't let me stay out late, it's because they really do care"). Then list some positive things that can happen if you soften, or give up, your position ("I might be able to talk with my parents better if I thought that they cared about what I want").

Stubborn position 1:

_____

Why I haven't been able to give it up:

_____

The benefits of softening or giving up this position:

_____

Stubborn position 2:

_____

Why I haven't been able to give it up:

_____

The benefits of softening or giving up this position:

_____

Stubborn position 3:

_____

Why I haven't been able to give it up:

_____

The benefits of softening or giving up this position:

_____

83

REMEMBER TO BE KIND

❄ Being kind to others can bring you genuine satisfaction. Some of your fondest memories probably involve acts of kindness, either by you or by someone else. Most of us spend time chasing things we think will make us happy. But good looks, achievements, and awards don't bring the kind of continuous, ongoing satisfaction that being kind does. Kindness ensures that you'll be more patient, more optimistic, and easier to get along with.

Get into the habit of being kind by practicing random acts of kindness—little things done for others without demanding or expecting anything in return. For example, put a quarter into a parking meter that's about to run out so that someone avoids getting a parking ticket. This is a small act, but a kind one. List random acts of kindness that you can practice in each of the following situations. Note how long it would take and what it would cost you.

Where	Act of Kindness	Time Spent	Cost
At school			
At home			
At work			

84

TAKE CRITICISM A LITTLE
LESS PERSONALLY

❋ Rather than being upset by criticism, take a step away from yourself and look for the grain of truth in what's being said— if there is one, you can learn from it, and it won't hurt as much. Remember, criticism says more about the person doing the criticizing than it says about you. Becoming upset and taking it personally can keep you from learning about yourself.

Has criticism bugged you lately? See if you can find the grain of truth in the criticisms sent your way. Fill in the appropriate blanks below with names or descriptions of whoever criticized you and what was said. Then search for the grain of truth. For example: "Dad criticized me by saying I don't do my chores at home. The truth is that I forgot to take the garbage out twice this week and twice last week."

1. _____ criticized me by saying

_____.

The truth is

_____.

2. _____ criticized me by saying

_____.

The truth is

_____.

3. _____ criticized me by saying

_____ .

The truth is

_____ .

4. _____ criticized me by saying

_____ .

The truth is

_____ .

5. _____ criticized me by saying

_____ .

The truth is

_____ .

If you were able to find the grain of truth in three or more of the criticisms, your mind is open to learning more about yourself from how others see you, and you're not sweating the criticisms too badly. If you can't find the grain of truth in more than two of the criticisms you've listed, you're probably more defensive than you need to be.

85

THE FOUR PILLARS
OF THOUGHT:
PILLAR #1, THE WHAT

✴ If you were to master the four pillars of thought, your life would probably be a lot less complicated. The first pillar, *what* you think about, is one of the most important ingredients of life. Your thoughts determine your feelings and behaviors and relate directly to the quality of your life. If you always think negative thoughts, your life will be filled with angry, frustrated feelings. Joy and laughter come from positive thoughts. You can decide to put aside negative thoughts and feel a hundred times better.

You can change your negative thoughts into positive thoughts. Look at these negative thoughts, which commonly occur to teens. Change each one to a positive thought. The more you practice doing this, the easier it becomes, and you can make a habit of changing negative thoughts to positive ones.

1. My face looks awful today!

   Change to: _____

2. I look fat.

   Change to: _____

3. Nobody likes me.

   Change to: _____

4. I'll flunk the math quiz for sure.

   Change to: _____

5. If I don't get a date for the prom, I'll just die!

   Change to: _____

Have you had any negative thoughts lately? Write each one down, and change it to a positive thought.

86

THE FOUR PILLARS
OF THOUGHT:
PILLAR #2, THE WHEN

✳ *When* you think about something is often as important as *what* you think. It's all in the timing. If you're in a terrible mood—angry, resentful, defensive—and try to think about significant issues or sort out your problems, the result could be disastrous. You may not be motivated to think about problems when your mood is up, but that's really the best time to do it. Pillar #2—*when* you think about things—makes you better equipped to handle your problems.

When is a good time to consider your problems? Put a checkmark beside the *whens* that you think are best to address negative topics.

_____ When I'm already upset

_____ When I'm sleepy

_____ When I'm hungry

_____ When I'm relaxed

_____ When I'm rushed

_____ When I'm done with all my work

_____ When I'm fighting with my parents

_____ When my friends and I have had a good time

_____ When I'm cranky

_____ When I'm alone and it's quiet

_____ When my siblings are annoying me

_____ When I'm fighting with my best friend

_____ When I'm sick

_____ When it's late

_____ When I wake up feeling good

Can you think of a time when you might be good at addressing problems and issues? Do you function better in the morning or are you a night person? Do you like stormy days or sunshine? Make a list of times when you might be able to address problems with a clear head. Refer to this list when you need to figure things out.

87

THE FOUR PILLARS
OF THOUGHT:
PILLAR #3, THE HOW

 If you try really hard to think of solutions to problems, you often can't think at all, let alone come up with answers. Frustration can lead you to take actions that you later regret. But if you relax, take a few deep breaths, and clear your mind, clear thinking will emerge. Experiment with Pillar #3—*how* you think—and see how easily certain issues will begin to resolve themselves.

Are you struggling for answers to problems? What would you do in the following three situations?

1. There's only one math problem left in my homework, but I just can't seem to get it done.

_____ I keep working at it—I have to find the answer!

_____ I take a break and go for a walk. Walking sometimes makes answers appear.

2. I'm at a party and I can't remember someone's name—and no one else can, either.

_____ I feel foolish and don't want to embarrass myself, but I ask again.

_____ I let my mind go—if I give it something to do and leave it alone, it will remember things.

3. I don't know how to patch things up with my best friend—we had an awful fight.

_____ I stew and worry while I pick up the phone and put it down, unable to think of what to say.

_____ I relax and relive some memories. I look through some old photos of us together having fun.

Have you ever come up with ideas and solutions in a bolt out of the blue? Sometimes we can find a certain activity or place in which we become so relaxed the answers start to surface. It may be in the shower, or watching a sunset, or walking through the park. Write about the times you got answers out of the blue—what were you doing when you got your answers? Could this be something you can do in the future?

88

THE FOUR PILLARS
OF THOUGHT:
PILLAR #4, THE FACT OF

✳ Thinking is automatic, like breathing. Recognizing the fact that your thinking plays a significant role in the quality of your life is what Pillar #4 is all about. If there's a possibility that your own thinking might be getting in your way, making you feel bad, or making things seem worse than they are, you can recognize that fact. Once you do, any negative thinking and "thought attacks" can fade away.

Is your thinking getting in your way? Your thoughts are just thoughts. Consider the following.

1. When was the last time you were very unhappy? Write about it, and write what unhappy thoughts were going through your mind.

_____

_____

_____

_____

_____

Remember, it is your *thoughts* that were unhappy, not your life.

2. When was the last time you were really stressed out? Why were you stressed? What stressful thoughts did you have? Write about it.

_____

_____

_____

_____

_____

Remember, it is your _thoughts_ that were stressful, not that your life was one big mess.

3. When was the last time you were very angry? Write about what happened and why you were so angry. What angry thoughts did you have?

_____

_____

_____

_____

_____

Remember, it is only your _thoughts_ that were angry—your life wasn't.

4. When you recognize the fact that your thoughts dictate your feelings, you can change negative thoughts to positive ones.

Think of a time when you felt each of the negative feelings below. Write about it.

a. Disappointment _____

b. Frustration _____

c. Jealousy _____

d. Anxiety _____

e. Irritation _____

5. Could you have turned those feelings into positive ones by changing your thoughts? Write how for each one.

a. _____

b. _____

c. _____

d. _____

e. _____

89

TAME YOUR ANGER

✳ You can't get rid of all your anger, and it may not even be healthy to do so. You'll still get angry, often with reason. But if you recognize where your anger is coming from, you can tame it a little. Don't get carried away in a fury that will immobilize you or ruin your life. It's okay to feel angry, but control it—you *are* in charge of your emotions. Often, understanding the source of your anger brings enlightenment. So when you get mad, really think about why you are stirred up—the object of anger may not be at all what you are truly upset about.

A great way to tame your anger is to count to ten when you feel yourself getting angry. Here's how.

1. Take a long, deep breath.
2. As you do, say the number "one" to yourself.
3. Relax your entire body as you exhale.
4. Repeat the process, saying "two" to yourself, then "three," and so on, up to ten.

Give it a try. With practice, you can tame your anger and clear your mind so that you can better see where your anger is coming from. Use this log to track times that you feel angry. Note whether or not you tried counting to ten, and record what happened in each case. You may soon see that counting to ten to tame your anger yields more positive feelings afterward.

Time I felt angry	Did I count to ten?	How I felt afterward
_____	Yes/No	_____
_____	Yes/No	_____

Time I felt angry	Did I count to ten?	How I felt afterward
_____	Yes/No	_____
_____	Yes/No	_____
_____	Yes/No	_____
_____	Yes/No	_____

90

DON'T BE AN
APPROVAL-SEEKER

※ Approval-seekers make the majority of their important decisions based on what they believe others will think rather than by following their own consciences, intuition, and intelligence. Only you know what's right and true for you. It's okay to get other points of view to help you make decisions, but you don't need the approval of others to feel good about yourself.

Are you an approval-seeker? Take this test and find out. Read all three answers, and select the one that best describes you. Write the point value beside the statement.

1. When I sign up for new classes at school, I

_____ always seek approval from others. (1)

_____ never seek approval from others. (3)

_____ might seek approval from a few people. (2)

2. If someone tells me that they don't like the new way I've chosen to dress, I

_____ get upset and ask other kids what they think. (2)

_____ get really bummed out and avoid seeing anyone I know for a while. (1)

_____ ignore her, because I like what I'm wearing and it suits me. (3)

3. A teacher tells me how much he liked the speech I gave at the school debate. I

_____ tell everyone about what the teacher said to me. (1)

_____ explain in detail to the teacher how I wrote and practiced the speech. (2)

_____ accept the compliment by thanking the teacher graciously. (3)

4. I have a great idea for a class fund-raising event, but it gets voted down. I

_____ feel hurt and vow never to make any suggestions again since mine are all so rotten. (1)

_____ feel a bit hurt but go along with the idea everyone has chosen. (2)

_____ understand that the other idea is easier to carry out and gracefully accept it. (3)

SCORING:
4–6: You're an approval-seeker and need the approval of others.

7–9: You're sometimes bothered by disapproval and sometimes not.

10–12: You feel good about yourself without the constant approval of others.

91

DON'T BE A
DISAPPROVAL-SEEKER,
EITHER

❊ It may sound odd, but some teens seek disapproval, particularly from authority figures, because they feel that it makes them independent. The truth is that the ultimate sign of maturity is making a decision, even if your parents would approve of it. Seeking disapproval doesn't keep you from being controlled by others, but rather ensures that others are controlling you. Freedom always comes from making decisions based on what's right and true for you, not based on what others approve or disapprove of.

Can you make decisions based on what's right for you? Answer these questions. Write the value of the answer in the space next to it.

1. Mom always wanted me to take dance lessons, and now I find that I'm interested in doing it. I

_____ sign up for classes because I can't wait to get started. (2)

_____ don't sign up because that would mean I was doing what Mom wanted. (1)

2. Some kids are going against the school dress code to see what they can get away with. I

_____ put on some "forbidden" clothes and join them. (1)

_____ keep to the code because I don't like wearing the forbidden clothes anyway. (2)

3. My parents hate body-piercing, so I

_____ head to the nearest parlor, grit my teeth, and get my nose pierced. (1)

_____ agree with them. It hurts, and I think it looks funny! (2)

4. One of my friends has a new motorcycle and wants me to go riding on it, but my parents are terrified of it. I

_____ say "No thanks," because I'm a bit leery of it, too. (2)

_____ say that I'm going to the library and have my friend pick me up at the end of the block. (1)

SCORING:
1–4: You're probably courting the disapproval of others.

5–8: You tend to make decisions based on what's right for you, and you're not out to upset any authority figures.

Make a list of things you do just because your parents or other authority figures don't like them. After you're done, ask yourself why you seek their disapproval. Do you think it means you're more independent? Are you afraid of being controlled? How do you really feel about what you're doing?

92

KEEP YOUR
SENSE OF HUMOR

✳ Teens, like everyone else, often take themselves and their personal dramas way too seriously. The result is usually pain, fear, and frustration. When you're feeling self-absorbed, you believe that life is all about you and that everything that happens is directed at or against you. Lighten up! A sense of humor helps you keep your personal dramas in perspective and will serve you well when the going gets tough.

Can you lighten up and keep your sense of humor? Think about these situations.

1. In a restaurant, a waitress spills a glass of water in your lap. Which do you do?
   a. Get angry, yell at her, make a scene, and ruin dinner for everyone.
   b. Understand that she is upset about what she did, laugh, and say, "That's okay, this shirt needed to be washed anyway."

2. You're playing softball and everyone is teasing you because you don't hit very well. But then you slam the ball into the outfield, and as you turn to run, you trip and fall right there at home plate. What do you do?
   a. Get up and run away from the field in total embarrassment.
   b. Get up, dust yourself off, laugh, and say, "See? I ran around all of the bases so quickly that you didn't even notice!"

3. Your mom or dad is busy getting ready for a big work presentation. You ask for help with something, but he or she is uptight and snaps at you. Which do you do?

a. Get angry and scream, "You never pay attention to me! Everything else is always more important!"

b. Realize that he or she wasn't really angry at you and say, "Whoops, you're in that heavy-duty work mode again. Let me know when you're done, okay?" Then you back off for a while.

Have you had any personal dramas recently that you wish you'd handled differently? List them here. Write down what you did in the situation, what you wish you hadn't done, and how you might have dealt with it if you'd kept your sense of humor.

_____

_____

_____

_____

_____

_____

93

ADMIT THAT YOU'RE WRONG—
OR THAT YOU'VE MADE
A MISTAKE

✳ We use a lot of energy to defend ourselves and prove our positions when someone thinks we're wrong. All the arguing, correcting, and attempts to get people to see our way puts a lot of stress and pressure on everyone involved. If you're wrong or you've made a mistake, why not simply admit it and avoid the entire hassle? The situation will be resolved quickly, and everyone can move forward and get on with life. It's one less issue you'll have to sweat.

Can you admit you're wrong? Think about the following.

1. Think about a mistake you made at home. Your parents pointed out the mistake. How did you react?

_____

Now, what if you had admitted your mistake first? How would you have reacted instead?

_____

2. Think about a mistake you made at school. A teacher told you that you made the mistake. How did you react?

_____

· Now, what if you had admitted your mistake first? How would you have reacted instead?

_____

3. You and your friends argued about something, and you insisted that you were right. But someone proved that you were wrong. How did you react?

_____

Now, what if you had admitted your mistake first? How would you have reacted instead?

_____

94

REMEMBER THAT EVERYONE
HAS THE RIGHT TO BE HAPPY

✱ Everyone *wants* to be happy. It's part of being human. Sometimes people do things that annoy you, but if you look closely, you might see that their actions are part of their search for happiness. You may prefer that others behave differently, but if you understand what's going on, feel compassion for others, and see the innocence in their behavior, it will bother you much less. Remembering that everyone has a right to be happy can be like a "mental shield" against taking things too seriously.

What's really going on behind people's behavior? Perhaps they're trying to feel better about themselves. Here are some behaviors that you may not like in others. Beside each one, write the name of someone you know who might be acting this way, and consider where the behavior might be coming from.

1. Brags about what they have. _____

2. Belittles someone else. _____

3. Compares themselves unfairly to others. _____

4. Points out other people's flaws. _____

5. Hurts someone's feelings. _____

6. Acts insensitively. _____

7. Behaves irrationally. _____

8. Makes snap decisions.　　　_____

9. Is sometimes cruel to others.　_____

10. Shows off.　　　　　　　_____

For each person listed above, think of some ways that you might try
to see the innocence of these people and avoid becoming angry or
irritated with them. They may just be trying to be happy. How can
you adjust your attitude to these people? Consider how you used to
react to them and their behavior, and how you might now react if
you see the innocence. Write down your thoughts.

_____

_____

_____

_____

95

GO WITH THE FLOW

❋ Everyone is familiar with this phrase, but almost no one does it! This is an incredibly powerful way to keep stress under control and stop sweating the small stuff. Instead of being rigid and uptight and insisting that life be a certain way, going with the flow accepts that life is constantly changing and evolving. Like the current in a flowing river, it's more difficult to swim upstream against it. But when you go with the flow, the journey is smooth and easy.

We never know where the flow of life will take us or what will happen. If you can go with the flow, it means that you can be comfortable not knowing what lies ahead. Take this quiz to see how well you go with the flow. Read each statement and choose the one that best describes you. Write the point value in the space before the statement.

1. My best friend and I have a serious blowout, and I don't know what's going to happen with our friendship.

_____ I don't stew about it, because that won't help things. We both need time to cool off. (3)

_____ I might worry a bit until we can talk again. (2)

_____ I can't sleep at night, because I'll die if she won't be my friend anymore. (1)

2. My parents have been fighting a lot lately, and I don't know what will happen next.

_____ I'm really worried that they're going to get a divorce. (1)

_____ I try to find someone to help them. (2)

_____ I figure that they're just working things out, and I allow them that. (3)

3. My friends talk me into going to a party where I don't know many people and don't know what to expect.

_____ I figure that I might have a good time or I might have a miserable time. (2)

_____ I can always have fun at a party, no matter who's there, whether I know anyone or not. (3)

_____ I'll probably have such a rotten time that I may as well not go. (1)

SCORE:

1–3: The flow knocks you for a loop! Tell yourself that things will be okay, because chances are they will.

4–6: You could work a bit on not being thrown by the unknown.

7–9: You really know how to go with the flow.

96

EXPERIENCE

DELAYED REACTIONS

✳ A delayed reaction is an intentional hesitation between the time something happens and the time you react. It's the opposite of a knee-jerk reaction, which is an automatic response. Time, even a small amount, has great healing power. Putting a little time between something that bothers you and your reaction to it can greatly reduce the intensity of your reaction and the stress felt by everyone. Delayed reactions help you sweat the small stuff much less.

In these exercises, compare how you would usually react to a situation with how you might react if you gave yourself some time before reacting.

1. A kid at school calls me a name. I usually

_____.

My delayed reaction might be

_____.

2. Mom or Dad criticizes how I dress or my favorite music. I usually

_____.

My delayed reaction might be

_____.

3. Someone brings me some unexpected bad news. I usually

_____.

My delayed reaction might be

_____.

4. I see my boyfriend/girlfriend talking to another girl/boy. I usually

_____.

My delayed reaction might be

_____.

97

KEEP IN MIND THAT AS ONE DOOR CLOSES, ANOTHER DOOR OPENS

Changes and transitions in life can be great sources of sadness, stress, loss, grief, and frustration if we feel that a door is closing or that a chapter of life is over. A comforting truth in life is that when one door closes, somewhere, another door opens. Instead of feeling regret or sadness at times of change and transition, knowing that new doors are opening to you can bring feelings of enthusiasm and anticipation for what lies ahead. Looking back, you'll find that whenever you ended something, you began something new. This is the way of life.

Look at these situations in which a door in life closes. Can you see a new door that might open? Write about it and what opportunities it might bring.

CLOSED DOOR:
Your family moves to another town, state, or country.
NEW DOOR THAT OPENS:

_____

WHAT MIGHT LIE AHEAD:

_____

CLOSED DOOR:
You break up with your boyfriend/girlfriend.

NEW DOOR THAT OPENS:

_____

WHAT MIGHT LIE AHEAD:

_____

CLOSED DOOR:
  Your best sports season ever is over.
NEW DOOR THAT OPENS:

_____

WHAT MIGHT LIE AHEAD:

_____

CLOSED DOOR:
  A beloved pet passes away.
NEW DOOR THAT OPENS:

_____

WHAT MIGHT LIE AHEAD:

_____

CLOSED DOOR:
  You graduate from high school.
NEW DOOR THAT OPENS:

_____

WHAT MIGHT LIE AHEAD:

_____

CLOSED DOOR:
　　The organization that you belonged to for years has to cease operation.
NEW DOOR THAT OPENS:

_____

WHAT MIGHT LIE AHEAD:

_____

98

EMBRACE THE ATTITUDE
THAT THIS, TOO, SHALL PASS

❊ It's been said that the only certainty in life is change. No experience lasts forever. Everything has a beginning and an end, without exception. The comfort you can take from this is that bad times and bad feelings won't last. Like everything else, they will have an end. You can trust this wisdom in all aspects of life. Rest assured that whatever you're going through, big or small, it, too, shall pass. When you're absolutely certain of that, it's easier to let go of things, especially the small stuff.

Life is a series of events, one after another. If you look at the events of your life, you'll see that they all passed, both good and bad. Try this exercise.

1. Write about the earliest happy memory you have. It might be of an early birthday or when you got your first pet. See if you can recall how you felt.
2. Think of something that happened around the same time that wasn't so good. Perhaps you got tonsillitis, or your family moved to another town and you were scared. Remember your feelings and write about it.
3. Now write about another good thing that happened after that.
4. Recall something else that was less wonderful, and write about how you felt.

As you can see, you've had good times and bad in your life. They came and went, always replaced by new experiences. Write about more experiences to reinforce this fact. You don't have to get everything in exact order. The idea is to see a list of the experiences you've had.

99

LISTEN TO THOSE
WAKE-UP CALLS

✳ Wake-up calls are experiences that often become turning points in life. They teach important lessons and often result in positive changes in behavior or ways of thinking. It's as if the lesson must be taught and we must learn it in order to wake up to our problems rather than ignoring them or pretending that they don't exist. You can become a better person by heeding your wake-up calls, learning from the experiences, and taking positive steps not to make the same mistakes in the future.

There are lessons to be learned in wake-up calls. Here are some examples of wake-up calls. Fill in the lessons and what the end results might be.

1. You fight with a sibling and it gets rough—he falls and breaks his wrist.

   Lesson learned: _____

   What now? _____

2. You're caught cheating on a test and are suspended from all school activities for a month.

   Lesson learned: _____

   What now? _____

3. A friend is hurt in a car accident—she wasn't wearing her seat belt.

Lesson learned: _____

What now? _____

4. You fail a class because you've been having too much fun and not studying enough.

   Lesson learned: _____

   What now? _____

5. You've coasted through practice, not really trying, and the coach has cut you from the team.

   Lesson learned: _____

   What now? _____

Have you had any wake-up calls recently? What happened? What did you learn? Write about your experiences.

100

CONTINUE YOUR

JOURNEY

※ You have the capacity to become kinder, gentler, wiser, happier, and more productive. You don't have to make giant changes overnight to avoid sweating the small stuff, but a change here and a change there will add up. If you've learned new things so far and been touched in a positive way, continue being open to what life has to offer. Make the end of this journal just the beginning of a happier, more peaceful you. Treasure the gift of life—and may your journey be long, happy, and filled with success.

What can you do to continue your journey of self-discovery and growth? Try some of the things below.

1. Study a musical instrument.
2. Take dance lessons.
3. Learn to paint or draw.
4. Volunteer at a local soup kitchen or homeless shelter.
5. Do volunteer work for a group that rescues homeless animals.
6. Try an exotic ethnic food that you've never tried before.
7. Spend the day with an elderly relative.
8. Plant a small garden, if you have room. If not, plant something in a pot and tend it.
9. Learn a foreign language. Be creative and different.
10. Go to an art museum.
11. Take a nature hike or go bird-watching.
12. Start a journal and try to write in it daily.
13. Practice yoga or meditation daily or a few times a week until you get the hang of it.
14. Tell someone "I love you" today. And tomorrow.

15. Write a letter to someone you've been out of touch with. Try to write regularly.

Are there things you would like to do in the near future? In the long term? Make a list, and plan to get started right away!